Kings of Peace, Pawns of War

Kings of Peace, Pawns of War

the untold story
of peace-making

By Harriet Martin

Foreword by Kofi Annan,
Secretary General of the United Nations

continuum
LONDON • NEW YORK

Continuum

The Tower Building, 11 York Road, London SE1 7NX

Suite 704, 80 Maiden Lane, New York, NY 10038

www.continuumbooks.com

First published 2006

British Library Cataloguing-in-Publication Data

A catalogue record for this book is available from the British Library.

ISBN 0–8264–9057–3

Typeset by YHT Ltd, London

Printed and bound in Great Britain by

MPG Books Ltd., Bodmin, Cornwall

Contents

For Oliver, Sebastian and Isabel, who gestated along
with the book

Foreword

Over the past 15 years, more civil wars have ended through mediation than in the previous two centuries. The United Nations can claim some credit for this, since in many cases it provided leadership, opportunities for negotiation, strategic coordination and the resources to implement peace agreements.

But, while the United Nations is an obvious point of reference for peace-making efforts worldwide – and could undoubtedly do much more in the future if, as I hope, Member States agree to allocate additional resources to the Secretary General's 'good offices' function – it claims no monopoly in this area. Several of the most successful mediation efforts have taken place largely or wholly outside the UN framework. And there will always be cases where, for one reason or other, the parties prefer a non-UN context. In the last resort, what matters is not who does it, but the fact that conflict is resolved and lives are saved.

Successful mediation depends on a wide variety of factors, over many of which the mediator himself (or herself) has little control: for instance, the comparative strengths of the parties to the con-flict, their perception of the way the conflict is moving, their state of exhaustion or fresh hope, the support they are getting from various external forces, and just plain luck. Yet, clearly, a skilful mediator, enjoying support from key elements within the inter-national community (the institutional form of which may vary from case to case), can make a crucial difference. There is an art and a science here, and a set of skills which may be in part intuitive, but can also be honed by experience. It is therefore surely in the interest of future mediators, and of those who stand to benefit from their work, that this experience should be shared and analysed. And it goes without saying that there are lessons to be learnt from failed mediation efforts, as well as successful ones.

The United Nations therefore has good reason to welcome this book, which focuses on the experience of six individual mediators who have sought to resolve particular conflicts in different parts of Asia, Africa and Europe – three of them working for the UN, four under other auspices.

The efforts of these different mediators have life-and-death consequences, but their daily routine can often appear as endless rounds of fruitless meetings, airport waiting lounges, and hours spent negotiating abstract *communiqués* or *aide-mémoires*. Perhaps in a very few cases – where there is resounding success – their efforts may be recognized; but for the most part, mediators work behind the scenes, quietly and with the full knowledge that success will bring praise for the parties, and failure blame for the mediator.

In recounting the triumphs and tribulations of its six subjects, the book passes some judgements which not all of us would necessarily endorse. But its greater contribution is the light it throws, by examining the approaches and dilemmas of these individual mediators, on the essential *practice* of conflict mediation. This will, I hope, promote greater understanding and support for this crucial task among the reading public.

In short, the book brings to life, for the reader, the world of the conflict mediator, with all its frustrations and all its hope. I hope that those who read it will understand better the peacemakers' task, and that this in turn will deepen and widen the worldwide constituency that peacemakers need to sustain them in their life-saving work.

Kofi Annan
Secretary General, United Nations
New York, August 2005

Author's Preface

The signing of a peace-deal is the first most people know of a peace negotiation having taken place. The high diplomatic pomp of such an occasion, complete with a carefully choreographed smile as former belligerents put down their pens and reach across the table to shake hands, belies years of long sweaty effort during which time these sworn enemies were most likely more keen to remain foes than become friends.

The transformation from adversaries to peace-deal partners is due to many factors specific to the historical and political circumstances of each conflict. But there is one element which each peace negotiation has in common, and it is an element of peace-making which is little understood: the conflict mediator.

This man – in high-profile conflicts it is 99 per cent of the time a man – is the lynchpin sandwiched between the two sides at the negotiating table and sandwiched further still between the negotiating table and the international backers of that peace mediation. Squashed as he is between so many interests, it is often an uncomfortable job. But a vital and fascinating one. For this is the coalface of international diplomacy, where the interests in the ending of a war in one country extend far beyond the region to distant capitals around the world.

The idea for this book came from an annual gathering of international conflict mediators which the Centre for Humanitarian Dialogue in Geneva and the Norwegian Foreign Ministry jointly held each year in a hotel just outside Oslo. This event is akin to a couple of days of rather jolly group therapy. While providing a forum for serious debate of conflict resolution issues, it is also an occasion where weary mediators can get those knotty problems off their chest, exchange tips, give advice, go on lovely boat trips on the Oslo fjord, and tell rather wonderful anecdotes. Anecdotes worthy of a book.

That was the start of the idea for the book. And in one sense this is a collection of narratives about an aspect of conflict and conflict resolution which has often been overlooked: the personal experience of the conflict mediator as he tries to pull the parties from the mind-set of war and face them towards peace. But over the months of research, and as I spent time with each mediator, their staff, and the diplomats and parties whom they meet daily, a common theme occurred: his paradoxical relationship with power. He is both the perpetrator of the mediation process, and also, very often, the victim of it.

Hence the title for this book. For every mediator hopes they will become a king of peace and get a deal signed. In reality, each one of them is, at some stage along the way, a pawn of war, used both by the parties they try to help and, in some cases, even the backers of the mediation who are supposed to be helping them. A successful conflict mediator needs the skills of a chess master to play each side off against the other while moving them towards an end in which both sides can claim victory.

Each attempt to end a conflict covered in this book, be it in Afghanistan, Indonesia, Sri Lanka, Iraq, Cyprus or Sudan, exposes how the mediator in each case is taunted by the parties' provocative ambivalence towards peace. Be they rebel or government, for those contemplating laying down arms, the stakes of the game are high. And they are prepared to play dirty in order to win peace at a price giving up war is worth.

Unlike the backers of the mediation who have money and threats to use as a carrot and stick to push the parties along, and unlike the parties at the table who are free to walk away at any time, the mediator is powerless. He has only his neutrality and integrity to trade on as he pushes the process through many months, and probably years, of games of bluff and cunning.

Because of his powerlessness, if he is to retain his place between warring factions, he has to have the humility of a priest. Yet there is no room for innocents in this game; with the duplicity and tricks of which parties are capable, the mediator needs an ego to match those of the wily warlords and presidents he is pitched against. He has to be both a leader and a pleader. So this job attracts some fascinating personalities: risk-takers who are able to manipulate, cajole, persuade and when necessary, seduce with charm.

In the final chapter, Antonia Potter from the Centre for Humanitarian Dialogue pulls together the themes and issues thrown up by the experience of the mediators and explores how they relate to the growing body of academic mediation theory. Both the Centre for Humanitarian Dialogue and the Norwegian Foreign Ministry left me to tell these stories as I saw them. And it is important to stress, because of the sensitivities surrounding every conflict mediation, that any views expressed and conclusions drawn are entirely my own.

Harriet Martin
Geneva
October 2005

1 The Seasoned Power-broker

Lakhdar Brahimi
Iraq; Afghanistan

Special Advisor to the UN Secretary General, Lakhdar Brahimi was born in 1934. A former Foreign Minister and Ambassador of his native Algeria, former Under Secretary General of the League of Arab States, and once a Front de Libération National (FLN) insurgent fighting French colonialism, he became the UN's most senior mediator. His UN career has seen him lead several missions in and to Afghanistan, Haiti, South Africa and more. As Under Secretary General for Special Assignments, he was responsible for producing the independent panel review of UN peace operations in 2000 (the eponymous 'Brahimi Report'). He was the US choice of UN mediator to appoint the Iraqi interim government in 2004, and before that to work out a power-sharing deal in Afghanistan following the routing of the Taliban in 2001. He is also responsible for having mediated the Taif Agreement in 1989 which ended the Lebanese Civil War while working for the Arab League.

Iraq, 2004

Lakhdar Brahimi pauses, shrugs, and sighs. A sigh as deep and long and knowing as his 71 years. Was he right to have accepted President Bush's request to go to Iraq and appoint an interim government? 'I am not sure I have an answer to that one yet. Let's say it was not obviously the right thing to do. I really don't know. I don't know.' Does he feel comfortable about the decision to go? 'No, not completely.'

On 22 January 2004 Lakhdar Brahimi had a meeting scheduled at the White House with Condoleezza Rice. Again the Bush

1

Administration would try and persuade this seasoned old power broker, who had been instrumental in cutting deals in Afghanistan after 9/11, to try and redress the deepening mess in Iraq. The Sunni insurgency was escalating; and the US administration was starting to doubt the loyalty of some of the exiles it had hand-picked to temporarily govern. Meanwhile the stalled Middle East peace process, coupled with the ongoing Iraqi occupation, continued to fuel international hostility towards the US. The Americans needed help.

Brahimi was not just a mediator of extraordinary depth and experience; he was something even more valuable in American eyes – a Sunni Arab. And it was hoped he might be able to gain the trust of the Sunni leadership. Moreover, simply because he was an Arab, so the US thinking went, it was hoped his involvement could somehow make the Iraqi occupation less unacceptable to the Arab world. But thus far, he had refused to go. They couldn't afford for him to say no again. So the meeting, which was originally scheduled with just Rice, was upgraded. President George Bush was there, as well as Secretary of State Colin Powell. Even the President's wife, Laura, put in an appearance.

Brahimi, who had watched with disdain as the US first invaded Iraq, and then attacked his organization for not supporting the invasion, had been expecting this. 'I had said to a lot of people that the day would come when the Americans who had ignored the United Nations, who were looking down at the United Nations and who said that the United Nations had become irrelevant by refusing to support what they were doing – that in spite of all that, one day they would come back here and say "please help". And that's what they did in January 2004. That is exactly what they said.'

His staff say the Bush Administration didn't just say please, they practically begged him to say yes. And he did. 'But even then I went there very reluctantly, it's not a secret,' he says.

Brahimi's job, in which Bush had promised him a 'free hand', would be to oversee the appointment of an Iraqi interim government to replace the Iraqi Governing Council, a group of 25 people which the US had hand-picked the previous summer. The appointment of the caretaker government which would oversee the running of the country until national elections in January 2005 was supposed to mark the restoration of sovereignty to the Iraqi people. On 1 July 2004, so the plan went, the Coalition Provisional Authority would cease to run the country, it would once more be in Iraqi hands, and the US role would have been downgraded to a military one, providing security.

One of his colleagues says that Brahimi was 'flattered' to be pressured into a job he did not want. 'But it was very distasteful for him to be in an Arab country under occupation. Not only that, but to be perceived to be almost in bed with the occupiers. Extremely distasteful. And as an old Arab nationalist himself, it was a very bizarre situation. He was against the war itself and he remains clearly and vocally against the war having taken place.'

In fact, in the months before the war in Iraq, Brahimi was so concerned that the UN was not being vocal enough in its objections that he rallied his fellow high-level colleagues into more openly protesting the pending US invasion. One of them said he was 'surprised' that Brahimi then took the job to appoint the interim government, but added: 'You know, Brahimi is very professional and practical when it comes to making such decisions. Although he is man of idealism and strong principles, he is driven by what he can achieve through *realpolitik*.'

It is not surprising Brahimi is 'not completely comfortable' about his involvement in Iraq. The interim government he ended up approving did little to move the country towards more meaningful self-governance. And despite the promise of a 'free hand', he ended up effectively rubber-stamping Washington's choice of government and, with it, the compliant regime they already had in place.

It was not until the process was complete, that it became obvious the US government had ridden roughshod over

Brahimi's attempts to make the new temporary government more representative and independent. All the way along in their public statements the Bush Administration, and President Bush in particular, was always supportive of the UN's number one mediator. When asked what the transitional government would look like, Bush declared: 'That's going to be decided by Mr Brahimi.' Just a week before the announcement of the new Iraqi government, Bush said: 'America fully supports Mr Brahimi's efforts, and I have instructed the Coalition Provisional Authority to assist him in every way possible.'

Brahimi's entry into Iraq in 2004 had marked the official return of the UN to a situation it had pulled out of in despair the previous autumn. This followed the deaths of 22 UN staff in a bomb attack on the UN headquarters in Baghdad in August 2003, including the head of mission Sergio Vieira de Mello.

Brahimi began his work in the spring of 2004, spending several weeks in the country talking to Iraqis from every corner of society – politicians, civic and religious leaders, academics and businessmen. This, according to his staff, is the Brahimi method. 'He places enormous emphasis on knowing what makes a situation unique. There are lots and lots of people with lots and lots of views so you have to listen to them all. He is a phenomenal listener,' says Salman Ahmed, Brahimi's Special Assistant at the time.

Another member of his tiny team in Baghdad was his spokesman, Ahmad Fawzi. He says Brahimi works on the principle of 'navigation by sight', meaning he makes no assumptions about what he will find. 'He will go in with an understanding but he will say in all humility, "I don't know enough about this issue".' He has known Iraq for 40 years but the Iraq of today was not the Iraq of yesterday, let alone 40 years ago. So he will have 20 meetings a day with between two and 200 people and he will listen to them all.

'He would assimilate all this and he would wake up in the morning and he would say, "Okay, everyone, knowing what I told you yesterday, I don't think that's going to work. Get me a meeting with Mr X, you know from that group we met ten days ago." So he is constantly ticking. And you watch him walking with his hands behind his back and his head bowed and you can almost see the brain activity going on.'

By April, Brahimi's extensive consultation process was starting to irk some of those already in power in the Interim Governing Council (IGC), who saw it might mean the demise of those already in power. Ahmad Chalabi, once the darling of the Pentagon, was one of them. He had deeply influenced the early policies of the US during the invasion of Iraq. He is widely considered to be behind a smear campaign against Brahimi which was supported by some in the Kurdish community. Chalabi, a Shi'ite, used the press to claim that as a former Algerian Foreign Minister, Brahimi came from a regime which had been sympathetic to Saddam's own Sunni-dominated Ba'athist regime. Furthermore, the Algerian government had oppressed its own country's Berber minority, and therefore – so their logic went – Brahimi would have no time for either Iraq's previously oppressed Shi'ite majority, or its probably even more oppressed Kurdish minority.

Those close to Brahimi say that 'he was extremely offended that he had lived his whole career without ever having given any thought to the fact that he was a Sunni until he comes to Iraq, and some spoilers use this as a weapon to defame his good name and accuse him of bias. These spoilers claimed he was against the Shi'ites, had a preconceived plan, and that he had a list in his pocket of the cabinet he wanted. He had no such thing.' Brahimi himself now dismisses the smears as 'silly', saying that people who were 'sniping' against him 'have other agendas that have nothing to do with the fact I am a Sunni'. Part of this 'other agenda' for Chalabi, who was later exposed for double-crossing the Americans by also being in the pay of Iran, was his well-founded fear that he would be excluded from the interim government. He was.

Chalabi's campaign was largely played out in the media, something which Brahimi rather coyly says he 'has no appetite for'. This needs to be clarified. He has no appetite for the demands the media make on him during a mediation. This is hardly surprising, since media speculation can be very damaging to delicate negotiations. He does, however, have a fine nose for using the media to his own ends when necessary. And in doing so, is unafraid of stepping from the diplomatic shadows into the political spotlight.

It was just about the time of this smear campaign that Brahimi took measures to bolster his public credibility in Iraq and beyond; and place a good deal of distance between himself and the US' own agenda in the region. On 21 April 2004 he said in an interview with a French radio station that Israel's policy of 'domination' was 'the great poison in the region' and that the US was 'equally unjust' in its support for this policy. When he was challenged about these opinions, which had infuriated the Israelis and the Bush Administration, and sent the New York UN headquarters into an apoplectic frenzy of diplomatic embarrass-ment, Brahimi simply replied, 'It was not an opinion, it's a fact.'

Brahimi did not stop there. As the pro-Bush *Washington Times* ranted on 28 April 2004, 'Mr Brahimi compounded the situation by claiming in an interview with ABC television's George Stephanopoulos that Israel's malevolent policies toward the Palestinians were undercutting his diplomatic efforts in Iraq. Mr Brahimi also criticized American military efforts against insurgents in Fallujah whose goal is to make Iraq ungovernable, and warned against additional coalition military operations against terrorist forces.' Parts of the US media may have been up in arms about his remarks but Brahimi was actually voicing concerns widely held in many European and Arab capitals.

Brahimi is the first to admit that timing is everything. And thus it was amid this media rumpus over his various remarks that Brahimi presented his proposal for the shape of the interim government to the Security Council. He said his aim was to restore 'Iraqi sovereignty and independence' by establishing a caretaker government of 'honest and technically qualified per-sons'. This proposal, for a government of technocrats, not politicians, was based, he said, on what the majority of Iraqis, whom he had spent the previous weeks talking to, wanted.

The plan received widespread public approval, even from the Bush Administration. President Bush was less than gushing in his enthusiasm but admitted Brahimi had 'identified a way forward to establishing an interim government that is broadly acceptable to the Iraqi people'.

But the artful political showmanship with which Brahimi had publicly regained his own 'sovereignty and independence' from the US agenda in Iraq was not enough for him to actually regain control of the job he had been appointed to do. It is hard to use the word naïve of Lakhdar Brahimi. He has few rivals when it comes to notching up experience in the underbelly of international diplomacy. But one man alone needs more than political adroitness when he is up against a superpower. If not naïve, perhaps he was just overly hopeful to think power could be democratized so early in an occupation; that the Bush Administration would support the Iraqi people's desire not to be ruled by those they saw as American puppets on the IGC; and that the IGC would, indeed, be willing to hand over power to a bunch of technocrats.

Brahimi certainly didn't lack international support for his plan to restore Iraqi 'sovereignty and independence'. In the weeks leading up to the appointment of the new government, several countries wanted to pass a resolution at the UN which would give the new government legitimacy and a right to veto military action by US forces. It was a move the Americans were desperate to avoid. US officials let it be known that only after the interim government was named would they let this resolution go ahead. But in case the Iraqi government ended up with just such a veto, it became more important than ever for the US that Brahimi produced the 'right' candidates.

Meanwhile, the press became obsessed with printing the names of Brahimi's supposedly favoured candidates for the post of Prime Minister and President. Brahimi's tiny team of four people, trapped in the Coalition Provisional Authority (CPA) head-quarters in Baghdad, dependent entirely on the US for media facilities, phone lines and computer access, did what they could to prevent speculation for fear of damaging the delicate process. But over in Washington there were plenty of people who were willing to keep the rumour mill churning in order to keep the story in the news.

Ahmad Fawzi said, 'It was quite amusing and, at times, irritating to read in the *New York Times* and the *Washington Post* news about what Mr Brahimi was doing. It appeared as if we had been briefing but we had not. Some of the information was either too soon to be announced or the timing was wrong – or it was simply wrong.'

One of the possible names for Prime Minister which both the *New York Times* and *Washington Post* got hold of from US government sources was that of the nuclear scientist Hussain al-Shahristani. He was a secular Shi'ite, who had spent more than a decade in Abu Ghraib prison under Saddam. Significantly, although he supported the removal of Saddam, he had opposed the US invasion of Iraq because he 'did not think an all-out war on Iraq was the best way of doing that'.

In the days leading up to the announcement of the prime minister, both papers asked the UN to confirm that he was a candidate. The UN persuaded the journalists to hold off going public with his name, not least because he was an ordinary citizen who drove his own car and had no security. Anyone involved publicly in politics at that stage was in danger: just days before the President of the IGC had been killed by a suicide bomber.

On 25 May 2004 Fawzi, without mentioning any names, said his boss was going 'flat out' trying to develop a consensus across a broad cross-section of Iraqi leadership. 'And, of course, the closer you get to your goal, the tougher the bargaining becomes,' said Fawzi.

But then the next day, in what one UN official called 'a very ugly, very problematic leak', the *New York Times* announced

Shahristani was 'a leading candidate'. The following day Shahristani withdrew his candidacy. He told *Newsweek* that even though he agreed with Brahimi that most Iraqis thought non-politicians like himself were best placed to prepare the way for credible general elections in six months' time, he had pulled out of the race because of 'the delicacy of the situation'.

By now it seems Brahimi was no longer alone in running the show. The *New York Times* reported that Brahimi was now selecting candidates jointly with President Bush's envoy in Iraq, Robert Blackwill. Two days after Shahristani said he did not want the job, it was announced that Iyad Allawi would be the new Prime Minister. He was a man little known among ordinary Iraqis, having arrived back in the country only after Saddam was toppled in 2003. The previous 30 years he'd spent in exile, developing, among other things, close links with the CIA.

Salim Lone, a former UN advisor in Iraq, writing for the *International Herald Tribune*, says it was an American deal struck behind Brahimi's back. 'Brahimi was not even consulted,' he says. Brahimi's staff stress he was in the room when the decision was officially made, but it seems the decision had already been taken before Brahimi got to that room.

Back in New York the Secretary General's spokesman, Fred Eckhard, was caught unawares: 'This is not the way we expected this to happen, no. But the Iraqis seem to agree on this name and if they do, Mr Brahimi is ready to work with them.'

Ever the pragmatist, after the announcement Brahimi himself would not be drawn on his exclusion. Saying he did not want to discuss the details of the appointment, he did observe dryly that 'no one is going to get 100 per cent of what they want'.

The story was pretty much the same when it came to appointing the President. The then President of the Governing Council, a US-educated Sunni with strong ties to Washington, Ghazi al-Yawar, got the job. In a press conference afterwards Brahimi admitted that it was the Sunni Adnan Pachachi, a former Iraqi foreign minister in the 1960s, and not, in fact, al-Yawar who had been selected as the 'suitable person for the post'. But because of the 'the media taking on this subject' and also some 'other problems', Pachachi had been forced to step out of the race. Pachachi was furious about the outcome. Alluding to these 'other problems', he claimed in the press that there had been a 'shabby conspiracy' against him. He said: 'Brahimi told me I had more support than anybody to be President. He said I was by far the most qualified person.'

Despite the evidence to the contrary, there was still one man who continued to claim that Brahimi had remained in charge of appointing the new government. President Bush, welcoming the announcement, said: 'From my perspective, Mr Brahimi made the decisions and brought their names to the Governing Council. As I understand it, the Governing Council simply opined about names. It was Mr Brahimi's selections [*sic*].'

Not even Brahimi was claiming this. Nearly a month earlier, in an interview with the US National Public Radio's *Morning Edition* on 3 June, Brahimi said that the new Prime Minister, Iyad Allawi, whom he described as 'close to the Americans', had not been chosen by Iraqis. 'I would like to say now that this is over that he was definitely not elected by the Governing Council. The Governing Council was informed that he had been selected and they clapped to approve this choice.'

The day before in a press briefing at the UN, Brahimi had demonstrated his exceptional flare for telling it 'as it is' in a remark which was splashed across the world's press. When asked by the *Washington Post* about how he felt his effort to select candidates had fared, he said: 'The fact is I was invited by the CPA which governs Iraq – the government of Iraq, I sometimes say.' Then he really put the knife in: 'I'm sure he doesn't mind me saying this, that Bremer is the dictator of Iraq: he has the money, he has the signature, nothing happens without his agreement in the country.'

Momentarily, Brahimi was again setting the Iraq media agenda. The phrase 'Senior UN Official calls the US the Dictator of Iraq' grabbed headlines around the world. The next question Brahimi was asked at this press conference perhaps illustrates why he felt the need for a little bit of playful revenge: did he think that the Americans had 'got the better of him'?

Although he seems at one level disappointed, Brahimi is too seasoned in the fickle game of diplomacy to be shocked by the way it played out in Iraq. And now he seems unriled by the fact that having been 'begged' by the Bush Administration to help, it then went about undermining any help he had to offer. He simply says: 'People always say that the Americans are using the UN. It's true. Absolutely true. They are our most important members. They pay so they can use us. That's what we are here for.' Rallying to his own defence he continues: 'But we also try to use them. So at the end of the day, how much have they used us and how much have we used them?'

One of the UN's own senior sceptics believes that the Brahimi foray into occupied Iraq was counter-productive. 'I don't think that Brahimi has helped Iraq at all, but I think it was very helpful to the Bush re-election campaign. One could argue that Bush was re-elected in part because of the transmogrification of the Interim Governing Council into a government. Iraq has been a disaster for the UN, so much more so than for the US. It's not a question of the security situation, it was a bad political judgement for us to be in Iraq in the first place.'

Brahimi insists he never expected an optimal result. 'What would be best in a situation like Iraq was not what we were going to get. We knew very well that what we would get would be different. The thing is, was it good enough for us to accept it? Or was it bad enough for us to say, no thank you very much? That is the difficult question. I think it was somewhere in-between. Ultimately we said: "we will go along with it".'

Although he had been promised 'a free hand' when he took on the job, the forces were already stacked against Brahimi: the IGC did not want to give up power: and neither did the Americans. After the announcement of Allawi's appointment, Brahimi had dryly commented: 'You know, sometimes people think I am a free agent out here, that I have a free hand to do whatever I want.'

Even though Brahimi, perhaps more than any other senior UN official, is prepared to take political risks in order to safeguard his public integrity, he argues that speaking out against the appointment of the government was not worth the diplomatic cost. 'You see, sitting on the outside it is easy to say "why don't you throw everything in and just go home?" But it is not that easy – just think of the consequences if we had said that "this government is no bloody good and we don't want anything to do with it." Look what it would have done to Iraq. Look what it would have done to the relations between the United Nations and the United States. Look what it would have done in the region.'

He reflects for a moment, staring out of his window at the UN's New York headquarters high above the grey East River. 'So for your personal comfort, there is a price.' He sighs once more, and sinks deeper into his armchair. 'But it may be too high.'

Brahimi and the UN
Against the backdrop of the purposefully pointed skyscrapers of Manhattan, the rectangular United Nations Headquarters has the blankness of a glassy envelope waiting for an address. Perhaps because no one really owns this vast site – it is one of those odd splashes of international territory which dot the world – no one quite takes responsibility for it. Since its birth in the late 1940s, it has never had a proper refit. Now it feels like a dusty museum to the postwar hope in which it was built. Along the endless cramped corridors of its 38 floors sit thousands of battery-farmed bureaucrats working long days on world peace, cooped up in a building designed to serve 70 members but now meeting the needs and ever growing demands of 191.

Even on the top floor, the sacred territory of the Secretary General, there is no hint of the 21st century. Come out of the lift 38 storeys up and there is no reception desk of pale beech and smooth azure glass; no chic black-suited receptionist posing tight-lipped beside a vase of pale lilies. There are no edgy gum-chewing bodyguards, obligatory Raybans on their heads, lounging around. After all, the Secretary General is not head of a government; he is not even head of a proper civil service. He is running a members' club. And one which its members often don't love very much. Certainly not enough to keep up appearances.

And so the last line of defence, or rather the first line of introduction to the Secretary General of the United Nations, is a slightly overweight security guard in an industrial blue uniform with rather dated pointy lapels. Turn left from here and you get to Kofi Annan. Turn right, and at the end of the corridor you will find his special advisor, Lakhdar Brahimi.

Within the hierarchy of the UN, Brahimi has a special status. It's not just that he sits at the opposite end of the corridor from the Secretary General. He is probably the closest thing the UN has to a national treasure. Certainly his inner court, who talk of him with a touching mixture of reverence and pride, treat him like one.

Perhaps this is because, as institutions go, Lakhdar Brahimi is older than the UN. And it shows. His horizons are broader and he has a robust instinct for the organization's limitations. And he isn't trapped by the essential powerlessness of the UN game. Despite the pressures to kowtow to diplomatic etiquette, in the UN Brahimi's style is not cramped. So while the softly spoken Kofi Annan takes endless political flak from within and without the organization, Brahimi openly says what he thinks, and yet manages to sail through the political storms he creates, with a regal shrug and wry smile.

This is probably because, as Brahimi agrees 'absolutely', he is with the UN, but not of the UN. When he came to the organization in 1993 he was already an established player in international diplomacy, having held the position of foreign minister in the Algerian government, spent the 1980s as the Under Secretary General of the Arab League, and much of the 1970s as the Algerian Ambassador to the UK.

What reads now as a classic establishment career path conceals his exceptionally tough political, not just diplomatic, experience: his political career began in Algeria fighting for a revolution and ended in the early 1990s trying to prevent one. In the 1950s he was engaged in what he describes as the 'anti-colonial struggle', as an active member of the Front de Libération National (FLN) which was fighting for independence from France; in 1992, when the Algerian military controversially seized power to prevent the democratic election of the Islamic Salvation Front (FIS), Brahimi, who was Foreign Minister at the time, was retained to sit on a six-man 'High Security' Council to continue governing the country, from which he shortly thereafter resigned.

Brahimi, with his tall elegance and neat grey hair, has the chiselled charm and patrician manner of someone who has long been treated with a great deal of respect. His claim to have a 'very peasant background' doesn't quite ring true. Further fuelling his aura of belonging to the elite was the marriage in 2004 of his daughter Rym, a former CNN correspondent, into the Jordanian royal family. Landowners, perhaps, but 'simple farmers' doesn't quite wash.

For all this, Brahimi is not aloof. In a rather grand and grandfatherly way, he is warm, sincere and disarmingly humble. He thinks before he speaks. And having thought, is unusual among his fellow mediators in often admitting he does not know the answer to a question. Although with his experience he probably knows more than most.

But his likeableness belies a disconcerting hardness in his dark amber eyes. At an awkward moment in a meeting he will disarm everyone with what one colleague calls his 'alligator smile', a smile so long and white and engaging that no one dares raise an objection. This man does not just know how to broker power – he knows how to wield it.

His political street-cred has given him an edge over other mediators who have mostly been schooled in the diplomatic division of power. Unlike them he has an insider's understanding of power, having fought for it; and fought to retain it. And it is an understanding which wins him the respect of his interlocutors. As one of his staff says: 'When rebels say, "You don't understand what it's like", he says, "Oh yes I do", after all he was an insurgent in Algeria. Or a minister says to him, "You don't understand what it is like being in a government at war." He says, "Oh yes I do, I was foreign minister when my country faced these kind of issues."'

Afghanistan, 1997–99 and 2001–03

By the time Brahimi arrived in Afghanistan in 1997, he had already notched up a clutch of tough missions with the UN. His first job had been to help oversee the first democratic elections in South Africa in 1994. A colleague remembers how Brahimi's entourage was leaving the lobby of their hotel in Johannesburg one morning when they heard gunfire outside. 'We all immediately hit the floor. Everyone in the lobby did, even the receptionists and his bodyguards.' Only Brahimi was left standing, like a lone tree in the desert, still reading the document that was in his hand. Afterwards, when they asked him why he didn't get down, he dismissed the sound of bullets flying as mere background noise, saying: 'In Algeria, I lived through much worse than this.'

From there he went to Haiti, Zaire, Yemen, Liberia, Nigeria and Sudan. As was the case for many of these troubled countries, the nature of the Afghan civil war which had rumbled on since the collapse of the Russian-backed Najibullah regime in 1992 demanded someone who could not just mediate between warring factions but between neighbouring states.

After more than a year in the country, Brahimi managed to go where no other foreign diplomat had hitherto trod. He got his feet under the table, or probably more likely on the mat, of Mullah Omar, the reclusive cleric who was head of the Taliban. Brahimi later said of the Taliban leader: 'He is very shy, soft-spoken, and still very uncomfortable about his missing right eye. He is also quite inflexible.'

He was not the only one. After only a few months on the job, and having canvassed the opinions of leaders in 13 countries, Brahimi's pessimism about the task in hand was evident in the Secretary General's report of November 1997 which concluded: 'It is illusory to think that peace can be achieved. How can peace be imposed on faction leaders who are determined to fight it out to the finish and who receive seemingly unlimited supplies of arms from outside sponsors? These people all enthusiastically proclaim their support to the United Nations peace-making efforts but at the same time continue to fan the conflict by pouring in arms, money and other supplies to their preferred Afghan factions.'

But he kept trying. In April of the following year, Brahimi managed to get the various factions, including the Taliban, together to talk in Pakistan, in a meeting known as the Ulema Commission. But this collapsed after little more than a week.

In the following months Brahimi changed tack. Unable to sustain negotiations between the warring factions he now started focusing on the external powers which were funding and supporting them. In July 1999, months of intense negotiation came to fruition in the Uzbek capital of Tashkent. In what became known as the 'six plus two' group, Brahimi managed to bring Afghanistan's neighbours round the same table: China, Iran, Pakistan, Tajikistan, Turkmenistan and Uzbekistan, plus the US and Russia.

On paper this produced the desired result: the Declaration on Fundamental Principles for a Peaceful Settlement of the Conflict in Afghanistan. In it Afghanistan's neighbours, cheered on by the US and Russia, agreed only political negotiations not fighting would bring about an end to the conflict, and because of this agreed to stop providing military aid and support to the various factions.

But just a week later, the momentary sense of achievement had soured. Brahimi remembers: 'We took everybody to Tashkent in July, and everybody agreed, and we had a beautiful Tashkent Declaration in which these eight countries, six plus two, said in so many words, "We are not going to help the parties wage war and we are going to talk to other countries to stop helping." Marvellous!

'From there I went to Kabul where clearly the Taliban were preparing an offensive. Very clearly. It was visible. So I went to Pakistan and begged the Pakistanis, saying: "This is not going to achieve anything. This will just kill more Afghans and destroy a little bit more of what little infrastructure there is left. Please help stop it." And they said: "You are right, it's stupid." I was sitting with one Pakistani official, and he was promising this when the offensive started. And I felt sick — I felt very sick.'

Thousands of young Pakistanis had been fighting alongside the Taliban. Having failed to convince the Pakistanis of the futility of the offensive, Brahimi then tried to use the involvement of their young men to persuade them to withdraw support for the Taliban as they had publicly committed to do in Tashkent. 'I said to them, do it for Pakistan. Do it for Pakistan, not for Afghanistan. What I was telling them was that there are thousands of Pakistanis fighting alongside the Taliban in Afghanistan, where you are supporting very, very conservative people, who are speaking of a jihad, against Ahmed Shah Massoud because he is a Kafir, an unbeliever. What are they going to say, when they come back to Pakistan? You are playing with fire, it's just going to blow in your face.'

This plea also fell on deaf ears. Brahimi recalls how in the end he resorted to trying to convince the Pakistani Prime Minister, Nawaz Sharif, that it was in his personal interest to stop supporting the Taliban. 'I told the then Prime Minister, there have been two attempts on your life already. How many are there going to be? One month later the poor man was thrown out. So it was in their interest.'

But none of this worked. The offensive against the Northern Alliance in the north of the country started on 28 July and continued for a month. Just as Brahimi predicted, it did not significantly change the balance of power on the ground, but it did leave in its wake more than 2,000 people dead.

The empty promise of the Tashkent Declaration, and in

particular the fickleness of Pakistan, as well as the indifferent support of the big players, led Brahimi to do something he has done only twice in his long career: he quit. His resignation, he says, was a question of principle. He had to make a stand against the insincerity with which the Tashkent Declaration was signed: 'From my point of view, when you get into this situation with people in which they sign something and the next day do the opposite, you have to do something to show displeasure.' At the time he resigned he seemed not to be making a stand, so much as a declaration of defeat: 'At this stage somebody like me has no role. I have tried everything I know and it has not been of much use.'

The Tashkent Declaration was supposed to have worked because it exploited the patron–client relationship between Afghanistan and its neighbours who had got together and agreed on a set of rules for peace. Such a system of leverage was typical of the way Brahimi tries to create new sustainable balances of power in warring states. It is more important, he says, than the form of leverage often resorted to by the international backers of a mediation whereby they threaten to withdraw support or try to induce a party into signing by dangling an enormous aid packages in front of them. Brahimi says effective leverage is about something simpler and more subtle: reassurance and status quo.

'Leverage is not about putting a gun to someone's head nor is it about promising something. It's about people who the parties have confidence in, who can reassure a partner that what is being proposed is not bad. And the implicit message is "Don't worry, we will continue supporting you, we will not give you up, you are not going to lose everything, you are making concessions that are acceptable."'

This type of leverage was as important as ever for Brahimi, when he re-entered the realm of Afghan power-broking in December 2001 once more as the Secretary General's Special Representative. This time he was bringing a much broader circle of international pressure to bear on the various factions in order to get them to sign the deal on the table. Many nationalities, including the Americans, British, Iranians, Pakistanis, Germans, Russians, Chinese and the French were all invited to get involved. 'They were calling the various players that they had relations with, to encourage them to move forward. So, of course, you need leverage,' says Brahimi.

In the case of Afghanistan, you also needed a US bombing campaign. In October 2001, the US had turned its post-9/11 wrath on the Taliban who were refusing to hand over Osama bin Laden, whom they had been harbouring, along with his Al Qaeda cohorts. The US was backed by Northern Alliance forces on the ground, into whose hands the capital Kabul had fallen by mid-November.

Just two weeks later – although Brahimi says US Secretary of State Colin Powell 'wanted it even quicker' – a peace conference took place in Bonn. The aim was to thrash out an agreement to establish a new united Afghanistan. Before Bonn started Jeremy Greenstock, the UK ambassador to the UN, was quoted as saying of Brahimi's mission, 'We've handed him a pretty large, over-heated potato. It would be a miracle for anyone to pull off what the Security Council has asked him.'

At the Bonn talks, which were held at the luxurious Petersberg Hotel, on a hillside just outside the city, four main groups were represented: the Northern Alliance, the Pakistan-based Peshawar Front; the Iran-backed Cyprus group and the Rome group which represented the former King Zahir Shah. Exploiting the politically transformed landscape which existed after 9/11 and the US pressure and determination which came with it, Brahimi achieved what he had struggled previously to do for two and half years, in just a couple of weeks.

The US might have been orchestrating the wider process, but Brahimi, using what he calls 'very simple techniques' controlled the style of the actual talks. 'We started by saying there will be no official meetings, apart from the opening. And during that we didn't allow speeches, because in speeches people take official postures, they speak to the television, to their own delegation, and this pins them in corners and they become prisoners of what they say.'

To avoid this, Brahimi spent most of the week talking to the parties individually. The main get-together took place on the last day of the talks, by which time a basic text of the agreement had been drafted. In those final 24 hours, Brahimi not only kept the delegations up all night, he did not move from his seat, not even to stretch his legs, go to the loo or get something to eat. 'I stayed seven and a half hours without moving from my chair. Some of the delegates went out and came back. But nobody dared to say: "I am going to sleep" while I was sitting there.'

It was another of Brahimi's 'simple techniques' and it worked. As the night wore on, the delegates wore out. 'At the beginning they would look at every comma and every word and then they would get tired and they'd go a little bit faster. It's like in any meeting, really.'

Despite his preoccupation with getting an agreement, Brahimi was still taking great interest in what was going on in the lives of his closest staff. His Special Assistant, Salman Ahmed, had been unable to come to the conference because his wife was about to give birth to their first child. 'Every day he'd phone me and ask for news,' says Ahmed. 'On the final day he called me and asked, "Did you get your baby yet?" and I said, "Yes, did you?"'

He did. The Bonn Agreement, announced on 5 December 2001, included an interim power-sharing deal, an agreement to create a new constitution and to hold elections in 2004. But it was premised on a commitment by all sides to leave their previous incarnations as warlords behind, disarm, and start operating as civilian politicians.

In a country like Afghanistan this was a mighty commitment; and one which set alarm bells going among many, not least because of the many interested parties whose voices were either not heard or not satisfied in Bonn. The Taliban were the most obvious. But there were also influential warlords who were quick to criticize the agreement the moment it was announced. These included the Northern Alliance military commander, Abdul Rashid Dostum, the governor of Herat, Ismael Khan, and

Gulbuddin Hekmatyar, a former mujahideen commander, who was once backed by Pakistan but then switched allegiance to Iran. Hekmatyar dismissed the Bonn talks as 'a US conference under UN cover'.

From Bonn, Brahimi moved to Kabul to head the UN Assistance Mission in Afghanistan (UNAMA), charged with overseeing the establishment of the new Afghan government and the implementation of the Bonn Agreement.

But much of his time in this new mission went not into negotiating with Afghans but with Americans. The US and Coalition military forces had their own agenda and it was not written in Bonn. Their primary task was to track down Osama bin Laden and any Al Qaeda activists or renegade Taliban forces that went with him. To do this they employed a tactic well documented by human rights groups and the press of using warlords to help them in the hunt. The Coalition forces' 'warlord strategy' was in theory supposed to support the Bonn process, by literally buying, sometimes with black plastic sacks stuffed with dollars, the various factions into the new government. But it threatened the very fabric of the Bonn agreement, a key pillar of which was the establishment of a single Afghan army.

This left those now ruling the country without a means of doing so. When the new Afghan leadership, backed by Brahimi, suggested NATO troops should move beyond Kabul to provide security, the US quickly blocked the proposal. Instead it suggested that the warlords should be used to provide security until the Afghan army was trained up to do the job.

His staff say that over the months Brahimi was actually quite successful in convincing the Coalition forces that the Bonn agenda was in fact a 'shared vision': in order to stop the country being a launching pad for terrorism, and allow themselves an exit strategy, Bonn could be useful to them too in getting a stable Afghan state. But even if Brahimi was managing to manipulate US policy on the ground, it never happened fast or effectively enough. And the insecurity of the country, fuelled by an ever-blossoming opium trade, was arguably worse after the Bonn agreement than before it.

Some of Brahimi's senior UN colleagues say that this was an inevitable result of Bonn having a quick-fix agenda. 'Brahimi's weakness was that he had tactics but no strategy. He was successful at devising the right tactics to produce a government from a negotiation process; but there was no strategy as to what the actual state of Afghanistan should look like. It was assumed, for example, that central government, a model which has never worked in that country, was the answer, when in fact some sort of federalism might have been a better solution.' Those who worked for Brahimi at the time say this argument ignores the fact that the Afghans were unanimous in rejecting any suggestion of federalism. 'And it could hardly have been forced upon them,' says one of his aides.

Some of those working in UNAMA also say that Brahimi lacked the more plodding practical skills needed to translate his brilliance at the negotiating table into producing a government as outlined in the Bonn Agreement. 'The Afghan government never really developed beyond anything more than a shell. Ironically, you actually needed someone more technocratic than political in order to actually establish institutions that functioned properly.'

Brahimi's staff argue that Bonn was an 'ongoing negotiation', and so long before state-building in Afghanistan could become a technical job there were endless political matters to resolve. So Brahimi found himself negotiating security issues with the Northern Alliance and mediating between the Supreme Court, Attorney General and Minister of Justice, rather than spending his time working out how to ensure each government ministry would function properly.

With his usual candour, Brahimi readily admits the deal struck in Bonn was far from perfect. 'We've been criticized, quite rightly, that we did not get the whole package together in Bonn. It was simply impossible.'

'Of course you aim for the moon,' says Brahimi. 'Why not? But don't say you are going to get to the moon today, if it takes several steps to get to the moon. This is what I call achievable objectives. Set achievable objectives.'

Brahimi's philosophy is that a peace agreement is unlikely to be a perfect solution to the whole conflict but should provide 'a means of stepping forward'. Does this mean he seeks peace at any price; is a bad agreement always better than more war? He pauses for a long time, a pause which sinks into a lengthy silence, before he replies that he does not know. And then he recalls his experience in mediating between the factions in the war in Lebanon which he helped bring to an end with the Taif Agreement in 1989 while he was working for the Arab League.

'In Lebanon the agreement we had was not very good but it ended a horrible civil war, and it did not aggravate the situation that existed. Maybe it delayed some solutions – a lot of Lebanese wanted the Syrians out, but it wasn't possible then. So if you keep the Syrians and have peace, it is better than having the Syrians and no peace.

'In Afghanistan, on the contrary, in 1999 I left the job because there was no way of even a partial step forward. I think what you try and do in such complicated situations is at the very least, not make things worse,' he says with an ironic twinkle.

Brahimi took this step-by-step approach to the Bonn process. As one of his close aides says: 'What was available at Bonn was an opportunity to reach an agreement on a transitional process, a process that was understood at the outset not to be fully representative, but it would lay out a series of steps to build more representative government and thereby to build legitimacy.'

These steps were an interim government, composed of groups represented at Bonn, which would, in turn, call a national *loya jirga*, a grand council representing Afghan groups from across the country, who would then agree on a transitional government. The transitional government would then oversee the drafting of a constitution and, in time, hold national elections.

These elections, when they were eventually held in the autumn of 2004, provoked their own whirlpool of controversy. The UN had decided that because of the declining security situation, parliamentary elections would be postponed. This was because in many areas which were still in the hands of warlords, they would not be free and fair. Instead only the presidential elections – which saw the interim President Hamid Karzai democratically put in office – were held on the grounds that they involved national candidates not local ones.

But the UN came under a lot of criticism for holding only presidential and postponing the parliamentary elections. This frustrated Brahimi. 'I said if you want to have both together then you have got to postpone both because having both now is repeating Angola. It is starting another civil war for ten years. But there is a chance of having presidential elections so let's have them.'

Brahimi says that for the international community elections have often been a knee-jerk response in post-conflict situations, a response which was 'embarrassingly excessive' in the 1990s. 'We had a kind of naïve belief that elections were the elixir which solves all ills. And that once you've organized elections you've finished the job and can go home. I think we know a bit better now. Holding elections are an indispensable part of the political process but on condition they come at the right time and in the right sequence.'

Brahimi believes this strongly enough to have taken a public stand on the issue over the timing of the Iraqi elections which followed the end of the six-month term of the interim government he had been involved in appointing. The Bush Administration was adamant that despite the continued chaos in the country and a level of violence in which often scores of people were dying each day, the elections would be held on schedule in January 2005. In a comment which made it clearer than ever that Brahimi was no longer associated with the US Iraqi agenda, he described the situation in the country as a 'mess'. Asked by a journalist if it were possible to hold elections in the current situation, he replied bluntly: 'If the circumstances stay as they are, I don't think so.'

Brahimi and human rights

Brahimi's bluntness does not just court controversy outside of the UN. The organization, which as the world's standard setter on human rights law is deeply idealistic in parts, has had to get used to him too. Unlike some of his mediating colleagues, Brahimi does not see it as his role to be both the deal broker and the one waving a copy of the Universal Declaration of Human Rights at the often unsavoury characters he finds himself opposite at the negotiating table. Not everyone in the human rights field has welcomed this. 'We have a lot of problems with human rights purists and people like that,' he says gruffly. He believes the work of those in the human rights field is 'indispensable and complementary' but separate from his own. It's not that he doesn't believe in human rights principles – he is a strong advocate of them – but it is not part of his public persona. He will raise human rights concerns, but he does it behind the scenes. In Afghanistan, he did this often, including with the Americans after 'one particularly nasty' bombing episode in Khandahar; and earlier, during his first stint in the country, with General Dostum, following a report from Human Rights Watch documenting a massacre of civilians in Mazar-i-Sharif in August 1998.

But when he is at the negotiating table these are not issues he pushes. This is because in his line of work the pressing issue is ending the conflict and you cannot do that without cutting deals with these people, many of whom have 'blood up to their elbows'. So he refuses to get involved in the debate over whether or not any of the parties should be prosecuted for war crimes. It is not for him to pass judgement.

'If you accept these kinds of jobs, you go and mediate between warlords, faction leader, bandits, all sorts of people, people whom the human rights purists want to see hang. What I tell them is "Let me finish, and then go ahead and hang them." '

Would he talk to anyone? Would he talk to Osama bin Laden? 'If I were to mediate between Al Qaeda and the United States, I suppose I would have to.' He laughs, his face creasing in delight at the thought of it. 'But we are not there yet, are we? And Osama would refuse to talk to me, you have to remember that,' he adds, sounding disappointed at this afterthought.

Brahimi established the principle of talking to everyone and anyone through trial and error while mediating peace in Lebanon where he had to deal with a lot of 'very, very bad characters'. 'A lot of my friends were asking me if I was going to meet a certain notorious militia leader. At first, I said "No, never." And indeed, for some time I refused to meet him – this was a man whose hands were really full of blood. A lot of others had a lot of blood on their hands but he looked the worst.

'But he was wanting to meet. And he did represent an important constituency. So one night, I just thought, why not? The difference between him and all the others is a difference of degree. And when I came to Beirut, I didn't come to Beirut to meet nice Lebanese. The nice Lebanese are in Paris. And so the next day I called him, and I met him, and he helped us greatly.'

So does Brahimi become friends with these thugs and war criminals whom he can end up meeting for hours at a time, not just over days and weeks, but over years? 'You create a rapport, friendship is perhaps a bit strong. You certainly try to ask about how their children are doing, or whether their old mother is still alive. But all in all I don't think you really get close. These people have interests, these people have a lot at stake – much more than you do. They will never forget that you are really after taking things away from them.'

How important is it that the parties like you? 'They will always tell you that they like you. They have to.' But, he says, the parties are usually a lot more sophisticated than they look. 'Very often you think you are manipulating them, whereas they are manipulating you. So that is why one shouldn't try to be too clever. Just do your job, and don't pay too much attention to the flattery. If people are resistant or angry it doesn't mean they are worse than the man who tells you how great you are.'

Is he often manipulated? 'All the time.' Does he ever

manipulate? Brahimi pauses. His bristly grey eyebrows lower as he reflects. 'Probably,' he says slowly. 'But I hope, I hope I don't try to trick people into things that they don't know or don't understand, and they wake up and find they have given away something that they didn't want to.'

The master mediator pauses again. And then adds: 'I hope I don't do that. I am not sure, you know.'

Selected sources

Reports
'Afghanistan's Bonn Agreement One Year Later', Human Rights Watch, 2003.
UN SG Report S/1997/894

News sources
'Land of fear where the one-eyed man is king', *Guardian*, 11 October 2001.
'Bonn talks: who is being heard?', *BBC News Online*, Wednesday, 28 November 2001.
'Brahimi receives great negotiator award', Havard Law School website, 1 October 2002.
'Afghanistan's Bonn Agreement one year later, West pays warlords to stay in line', *Observer*, 21 July 2003.
'Bush lends support to the UN proposal for Iraq', *Associate Press*, posted on *Columbia Daily News* website, 16 April 2004.
'Bush's Brahimi gamble', *Wall Street Journal*, 20 April 2004.
'Brahimi's flawed policies', *Washington Times*, 28 April 2004.
'Scientist jailed by Hussein is favored for premier's post', *New York Times*, 26 May 2004.
'The man who won't be prime minister', *MSNBC.com Newsweek Web Exclusive*, 28 May 2004.
'Exile with ties to CIA is named Premier of Iraq', *New York Times*, 29 May 2004.
'US forced Allawi on UN, Iraqis: *NY Times*', *Islam on Line.net* report of the above *New York Times* article, 29 May 2004.
'Brahimi Explains Politics Behind Iraq Government Posts', *NPR Morning Edition*, 3 June 2004.
'Candidate who pulled out blames Chalabi Plot', *Guardian*, 4 June 2004.

Briefings

President Bush's Speech to officers at the Army War College in Carlisle, *Inter Press Service*, 25 May 2004.

White House Rose Garden press briefing, 1 July 2004, cited at www.pbs.org/newshour/bb/white_house/jan-june04/iraq_06–01.html

UN press briefing on Iraq, page 5/16, 3 June 2004.

UN press briefing by Special Envoy to Afghanistan, 20 October 1999.

2 The Chess Master

Alvaro de Soto
Cyprus

Alvaro de Soto joined the United Nations in 1982, on secondment from the Peruvian Diplomatic Service for whom he had served in the Peruvian Permanent Missions to the UN in New York (1968–75) and in Geneva (1978–81). He was the coordinator and negotiator of the Group of 77 in the UN Conference on the Law of the Sea (1974–82). In the UN he served in the Executive Offices of Secretaries General Javier Pérez de Cuéllar and Boutros Boutros-Ghali from 1982 to 1993. He led the 1990–91 negotiations which brought an end to the war in El Salvador. He was Assistant Secretary General for Political Affairs from 1994 to 1999 and was the Secretary General's Special Adviser for Cyprus from late 1999 until late 2003, and again from February to June 2004. He took over as Special Representative of the Secretary General for the Western Sahara in October 2003. In May 2005 he was appointed Special Coordinator for the Middle East Peace Process and Personal Representative of the Secretary General to the Palestine Liberation Organization and the Palestinian Authority.

There is a much-loved BBC radio quiz show called *Just a Minute* where contestants have to talk on a given subject from hairdressing to hieroglyphics for 60 seconds without hesitation, deviation or repetition. President Rauf Denktash of the as-yet-unrecognized Turkish Republic of Northern Cyprus (TRNC) would make a rather good contestant. As a British-trained barrister with 30 years' experience in the presidential role, he has mastered the essential technique: he does not deviate from his subject and he talks without hesitation. But there is a slight hitch. He has to talk about a *diverse* range of subjects and he only has one (Cyprus) and then there is also the question of repetition...

Forty minutes into the interview his monologue has been interrupted only once. The question was aimed at getting him to talk about Alvaro de Soto's mediation which began in 1999 and ended in failure in 2004 when a referendum outlining a plan for reunification was rejected. But it is roundly rejected when the President, who had begun with Cypriot independence in 1960, gruffly responds: 'But we are only at 1974.' Cyprus has the reputation as a mediator's graveyard and it is easy to see why. If posing questions in an interview is this hard, it's not difficult to see how Denktash would have struggled to enter into the dialogue necessary for negotiation.

It is not that Denktash is so prickly. He is actually very likeable. He is warm, ebullient, and has an endearing rotundness which gives him the sweet look of a teddy bear. And he's clever and witty. But he does go on.

More than two hours later, the tapes had run out, as had the will to ask questions, even the will to listen. When complete defeat lay self-evidently before him, Denktash finally got up, brushed himself down a little, and came round from the other side of his desk with a smile on his face, offering a friendly hand to shake before saying goodbye. It only then became clear how short he was. And, more alarmingly, that he was as wide as he was tall; a man, if it came down to it, physically capable of blocking progress. Since the 1970s the international community had spent millions of dollars and diplomatic man-hours trying to solve the Cyprus problem, but with all the will in the world, there was no way around Denktash.

An audience with the indomitable Denktash raises one rather interesting question. Over five years Alvaro de Soto spent hundreds, probably thousands, of hours listening to this to man. How did he do it?

The answer is, he fell asleep. Not often and only *in extremis*. On those rare occasions when the superhuman patience for which he is renowned ran out. And he did it with an exquisite sense of diplomacy that only someone with the knowing charm of this dapper Peruvian diplomatic could muster. For it was an impartial response. On occasion, he would drop off listening to Greek Cypriots too. Both sides complain of this, but it is a complaint tinged more with affection than indignation.

In general though, de Soto's response to the challenges of mediating Denktash were far more sophisticated than napping. He was conscious from the outset of the enormous obstacle Denktash presented to finding a solution in Cyprus. Twenty years after declaring the Unilateral Declaration of Independence (UDI), and after 30 years as President, Denktash wanted only one solution: the recognition of his independent state. Despite international envoys repeatedly explaining to him this would not happen, Denktash, who had built a presidential career on this promise, would not give up.

Cyprus became a divided island when in 1974 the Turkish army invaded the north following a Greek-backed coup in Nicosia. The Greek Cypriot army officers who had seized power did so with the aim of achieving *enosis* – union with Greece. Turkey sent in its troops in order to protect the Turkish Cypriot minority, which today constitutes less than 20 per cent of the total Cypriot population of 800,000.

In the wake of the invasion, thousands of Greek Cypriots abandoned their homes and fled south, where they have lived as refugees for nearly three decades. During this time Turkey encouraged thousands of people from the mainland to settle in the north, while maintaining a significant military presence on the island. From the time of its invasion, Turkey established itself as the financial and military backer of Denktash's kingdom in the north. But lack of recognition brought with it economic and political isolation from the rest of the international community and over the three decades it was the south which prospered. Today, Greek Cypriots have an income three or four times higher than those living in the north.

Alvaro de Soto

Since 1974 the international community had tried repeated mediation attempts to resolve what is known domestically as the Cyprus *issue*, but to no avail. In 1999 there was reason to hope that one more attempt would pay off. In that year at the European Union (EU) Helsinki summit, Cyprus was granted entry into the accession process. Turkey, although still a long way behind, got on the first rung of the ladder with the EU agreeing to consider its application. At that time it was unthinkable that the EU would allow a country locked in an ongoing dispute over its territory to become a member of its club. So the prospect of EU membership provided a real incentive to both sides to make this new round of mediation a success.

The only problem was Denktash. Unlike the vast majority of his population, he didn't give a fig about joining the EU. What he cared about was getting his sovereignty. This was one of the many challenges facing Alvaro de Soto when, in the autumn of 1999, Secretary General Kofi Annan appointed him as his Special Envoy to try and resolve the Cyprus issue.

Presented with Denktash's famed intransigence, de Soto artfully navigated an entire mediation around him. He negated his refusal to find a compromise solution by producing one himself, and then quashed his right to object to it, by invoking the highest principle of democracy and holding a referendum and letting the people decide. As it turned out, though, it was not Denktash's intransigence that was in the end the problem.

It was a question of timing. In the last stage of the process, the international community's prayers were answered when Denktash was replaced at the negotiating table. True to form, Denktash had spent the first four years of the mediation saying 'no' to any solution de Soto had come up with. In the final round of talks with the knees of his replacement, the pro-European, pro-reunification Mehmet ali Talat, firmly under the negotiating table, things should have been looking up for mending the Cypriot divide. But by that time things had changed on the Greek Cypriot side.

32

The long-serving President Glafkos Clerides, who supported the UN's peace efforts, had been kicked out. To begin with, his replacement, the wily Tassos Papadopoulos, didn't seem to be a cause for too much concern. Even though politically he was a Greek Cypriot hardliner, traditionally opposed to reconciliation attempts, he said 'yes' to the plan for reunification all the way along. Until, that is, at the final round of talks, faced with the absence of Denktash, there was no one to say 'no' for him. So Papadopoulos had to say it himself.

Indirect Talks, 1999–2000

What de Soto later called 'the biggest diplomatic effort the UN has ever undertaken, on any issue' got off to a slow start. In the first two years of the talks there was little tangible progress. At the end of 1999 the process had started with proximity talks because Denktash, right on cue, refused to meet Clerides until he was 'recognized as the President of a State'. By the summer of 2000, de Soto had had hundreds of hours of meetings with both sides individually. Even though neither side perceived the process to be moving forward, for de Soto the time had not been wasted. Using the copious notes his team had taken during each meeting, he started to come up with possible solutions on each issue. These tentative proposals were then subtly thrown into the talks, and each party's reaction carefully gauged. In the autumn of that year, as new ideas were gradually aired, the process picked up some momentum. Denktash responded predictably. He walked out. By this time, de Soto's team had already come to the conclusion that the only thing the Turkish Cypriot President feared more than a bad agreement was a good one.

With Denktash still in a huff, for most of 2001 no talks took place. De Soto kept busy evolving the basis for what would become a Comprehensive Settlement of the Cyprus Problem, known commonly as the Annan Plan, after the Secretary General, Kofi Annan, who acted as the patron of the process. But it was not until the end of 2001 that de Soto's mediation, which had begun two years earlier, really got started. By then the Turks were getting edgy, knowing that their own progress in the EU accession process would be affected by the lack of progress on Cyprus. So under Turkish pressure Denktash returned to the process, and this time he was prepared to talk face to face with Clerides.

Direct talks, 2001

Both now in their eighties, Clerides and Denktash go back a long way. There can be few political leaders in the world who rival their experience at the negotiating table. They have sat opposite each other in repeated mediation attempts. Even though political adversaries, over the years their familiarity with one another evolved into a touching friendship. With or without formal talks taking place, they always kept in touch. In the midst of tense negotiations in 2002, Denktash was in New York recovering from open heart surgery and Clerides phoned to wish him a speedy recovery. Denktash told him: 'Glafkos, I wouldn't wish this on my worst enemy.' To which Clerides replied: 'Thank you, Rauf.' Denktash responded: 'Don't make me laugh, it hurts my stitches.'

Their humour helped oil de Soto's process. At awkward moments when it seemed one or other side would walk out, one of them would crack a joke at the other's expense and get everyone laughing. Having refused to talk face to face to Clerides at the start of de Soto's mediation, Denktash actually asked for the direct talks to exclude de Soto so that he and his old adversary could sort out their problems in a 'heart to heart' like old friends. Clerides insisted in keeping the UN involved. So Denktash relented to allow de Soto to sit in as a 'fly on the wall'.

Michaelis Papapetrou, Clerides' legal advisor, says that despite Denktash's attempts to limit de Soto's role to a walk-on part, he ended up playing the lead. In the early stages Denktash told de Soto that he was not allowed to speak, he could only listen. Papapetrou says: 'Denktash said: "Your presence here amounts to a picture hanging on the wall, you say nothing, you are not part of the process." And de Soto patiently smiled and said nothing. But step by step he established himself not only as part of the process, but as the protagonist of the process.'

At the first meeting between the two sides, Clerides complained that Denktash was talking about his vision of a united Cyprus and not the practicalities of how to achieve it. Denktash responded by saying: 'If we haven't got a common vision, how can we ever agree on anything?' It was a typical Denktash tactic. As Robert Dann, one of de Soto's right-hand men, says: 'Clerides was prepared to negotiate, whereas Denktash was not. He would only state and restate his position.'

Alvaro de Soto had anticipated this. He knew that, because of their own political constituencies, both sides would find it difficult to make the concessions necessary to allow the process to progress. On the other hand, neither side wanted to be blamed for holding it back. It was this razor-thin discrepancy that de Soto spent the mediation trying to exploit.

He says he told the Secretary General early in 2002 that the UN would have to formulate its own reunification plan because 'these chaps are never going to come up with it'. But it was vital that they didn't do this heavy-handedly. 'We had to give them enough time though, so there could never be any accusation that we muscled ourselves in,' says de Soto.

Dann remembers how for most of 2002 de Soto waited for his moment. 'Part of the de Soto strategy was not to impose himself on the parties, but to make their non-progress prove that unless the UN came up with a plan, this whole thing couldn't go anywhere.' It took nearly a year and around 50 meetings for the parties to talk themselves to a standstill. 'By this point,' says one of the UN team, 'everyone but Denktash was practically begging us to put something on the table because they knew they could never come up with something themselves.'

Underneath this waiting-it-out strategy was a second line of attack. While de Soto sat at the table with the principal negotiators, he had members of his team testing out ideas, not yet officially put forward, on their advisors. This meant that by the time these ideas were dropped into the formal talks, no one was too shocked, as both parties had been 'primed'.

Papapetrou says it was only in retrospect that they realized de Soto was not just pushing the negotiation forward, he was moulding it every step of the way. 'He would add one small pebble one day, and then fifteen days later, he added another. By this point the interlocutors would have forgotten about the first one, and how it related to the second. It was only when we saw the plan that we understood the rationale and logic behind it,' says Papapetrou, giving the example of how he dealt with property rights. On one occasion, de Soto acknowledged the right of owners to reclaim the property they had lost in 1974. On another, he would start suggesting exceptions to this. In another meeting he proposed incentives for people to give up this right on a voluntary basis. 'It was only when all these pebbles were put together we realized it was a plan!'

De Soto accepts this was a case of finding a solution through consultation rather than negotiation. 'We got their reactions, we tried to accommodate them, and then make revisions to the plan on that basis.' Clerides, too, initially resisted this approach. On one occasion he said to de Soto: 'Mr de Soto, with all due respect I want to negotiate with Rauf, not you.' And de Soto laughs as he remembers how he replied: 'Well I may be the best you can get.' De Soto says in the end he had to level with the parties, admitting he was devising his own plan. 'At some point, I told them: "The way this is going you chaps aren't likely to agree to anything and we will have to put something before you." Clerides accepted this, but Denktash groaned.'

With Denktash as a sparring partner, Clerides comes across as a moderate and reasonable man. Over tea in his drawing room, surrounded by silver-framed photos of himself with the British royal family, he says de Soto worked by 'not telling Mr Denktash what I was thinking, and by not telling me what Mr Denktash was saying or how far he was prepared to go'. But wasn't de Soto at a disadvantage because Clerides and Denktash go back such a long way? Clerides, who as Head of State had known his fair share of mediators, chuckles and takes another sip of tea. 'I am sure both Rauf and I could see through it. But de Soto had to try.'

Alvaro de Soto comes breezing into the little Italian restaurant in Brussels with the air of a theatre director taking a break from rehearsals. His tweed jacket, yellow cashmere scarf, shaved head, and vaguely unshaven face makes it look as if the UN has produced its own version of Sean Connery. He is currently having a few days off his new assignment in Western Sahara – a conflict which the former US Secretary of State James Baker had recently given up on in exasperation – to present a paper on what went wrong in his previous effort in Cyprus.

De Soto is technically Peruvian but to a Brit seems about as Peruvian as Paddington Bear. Although he speaks with a mid-Atlantic accent, a product of a life in the international goldfish bowl, his vocabulary is charmingly, archaically British. He refers to the long line of interlocutors he has dealt with, be they rebels, war criminals, or ruthless hardliners, as 'chaps' and 'fellows'. And when they overstep the mark he accuses them of nothing more than 'bad form'. It's a legacy, he says, of British teachers at the International School in Geneva. Even though he left there 40-odd years ago, he still faithfully attends his school reunions. For a man who spends much of his life on a plane, the rootedness he still feels in the company of his old classmates remains 'very very important' to him.

Like many of his UN colleagues, de Soto is so international he is essentially nationless. He arrived with his family in Geneva after his father, a Peruvian diplomat, fled a coup in 1948 and took a job at the UN. Like his father, de Soto tried his hand at Peruvian diplomacy but ended up at the UN. Had he been more Peruvian, one imagines he might have entered domestic politics, but for someone who grew up trilingual in a city which is a no-man's land for nationality, the UN proved a more natural home.

During his career he has been a firm advocate of the high principles of the organization. He established himself as a skilled mediator early in his UN career when in 1991 he successfully brokered a peace agreement which ended the civil war in El Salvador. By 1999 Kofi Annan was asking him to draw up guidelines for fellow mediators to use.

Despite his standing in the organization, he is not a typical UN bureaucrat, by any means. His passion for literature and language gives him an uncommonly playful edge, and his love of words and wordplay is a tool he uses to stretch diplomatic etiquette until its elastic threatens to snap. One long-time colleague says he is 'charming and arrogant' in equal measure, and 'does not wince from being ruthless when necessary'. As both his admirers and detractors will tell you, de Soto is a 'very clever man'.

In this sense, the Cyprus mediation suited de Soto perfectly. This was a process that, lacking the emotive passions of an active war to end, was driven not from the heart but from the head. It was an intellectual exercise which de Soto approached with the calculating coolness of a chess master. In fact all the protagonists, de Soto included, talk quite unconsciously about this mediation as a game, describing their fellow players in terms of how they understood or did not understand its rules.

Over coffee and nougat ice-cream, de Soto reflects on what went wrong in the final phase when the Greek Cypriots rejected his plan at referendum. And he comes out, as he commonly does, with a Shakespearean quote: 'The first thing we do, let's kill all the lawyers.' Had they followed this advice, there would have been no mediation. Everyone involved was a lawyer. In fact, a law degree seemed a necessity to qualify as a participant. Denktash, Greek Cypriot President Glafkos Clerides, and his successor, Tassos Papadopoulos, were all British-trained barristers. It is said that Papadopoulos is 'one of the best contract lawyers in the English-speaking world'. De Soto himself is a lawyer and surrounded himself with a team packed with them. The result was a mediation which did not focus on the big picture, or as Denktash would have called it, 'a common vision'; instead the key to unlocking the Cyprus issue would be found in some rather clever small print.

The Annan plan

The first version of the Annan plan, as it became known, was presented to the parties in November 2002, nearly a year after direct talks had begun. Denktash puffs up indignantly as he remembers the occasion. 'And all of a sudden this "fly on the wall" produced a document of hundreds of pages.' De Soto laughs affectionately when told that Denktash says he had no inkling a plan was being hatched. 'The thing is Denktash is such an extraordinary actor that it is very difficult to tell what he genuinely believes and what he doesn't.'

There are certain things which Denktash unquestionably did believe. This is clear because he repeated them so often. They include the notion that Cyprus is an island made up of two peoples. In his eyes, since the Greek Cypriots had threatened to cancel power-sharing arrangements with the much smaller Turkish community in 1963, they had forfeited the right to govern them. Hence the need for separate states. Clerides, on the other hand, sees Cyprus as an island of two communities which should remain, as the British bequeathed it in 1960, one republic.

The marriage of these two philosophies was both the brilliance and the brittleness of de Soto's Annan Plan. At the heart of this was the concept of the 'virgin birth' of a new Cyprus, which the UK envoy, David Hannay, has summarized as a 'politically new but not legally new Cyprus'. De Soto, again taking divine pleasure in his choice of words, says it was not a question of creating a new state, but a 'new state of affairs'. The United Cyprus Republic would keep its current international identity. It would, for example, not need to reapply for membership at the UN. But under the plan it would be made up of two constituent states, with a federal government representing it internationally. The federal government, which would be governed by a collective presidency, would deal with only with the bare essentials of Cyprus' new international persona (foreign policy, defence, international banking, etc.). In principle, this solution meant that both sides could argue they had achieved their key goal. 'And that was the beauty of this very complex thing,' says de Soto, still marvelling at the cleverness of it. But not everyone saw it that way.

'And so I challenged de Soto. What is this "virgin birth"?' says Denktash, puffing up again. De Soto replied: 'The virgin birth theory allows the Greek Cypriots to argue to their people that the Republic of Cyprus is continuing. And it allows you to tell your people that your Turkish Republic of Northern Cyprus is continuing.'

But at this stage, convincing the people was not the issue. De Soto had to convince their leaders first. Clerides and the Turkish government had both accepted the 'virgin birth' notion. 'The problem was getting Denktash to play the game,' de Soto says. He wouldn't. Denktash says he told de Soto: 'You are not settling the problem, you are consolidating it in this phrase of virgin birth. After you have left, declaring to the world that you have settled the problem, we will still be quarrelling about it.'

What Denktash seems unaware of, despite a lifetime spent demanding an independent state, was that de Soto was his best and without a doubt, his last, hope. The international diplomatic community doesn't take kindly to people calling themselves President and creating their own new country. Denktash more than anyone knew this: in 20 years since declaring UDI, only Turkey had recognized his TRNC. 'The number of times I told him that what you are proposing is simply not going to fly,' sighs de Soto.

Despite this, de Soto spent many hours with Denktash trying to figure out how close he could come to getting him what he wanted at the negotiating table. 'I used to say to him, now listen, what is it about sovereignty which is so important to you. For me it's a theological term – it means they can't take away your rights –

and I can give you that without actually using the term. I can do that. We can make it iron-clad.'

De Soto's solution again rested on some skilful wordplay. To get around the fact that granting Denktash's little republic sovereignty was 'never going to fly', he invented the term 'sovereignly'. The Turkish Cypriot constituent state would be governed sovereignly, while sovereignty remained at the level of the republic.

De Soto's legal advisor, Didier Pfirter, a secondee from the Swiss Foreign Ministry, who had been the brain behind legally finessing this term, used press interviews to sell the idea, explaining it was based on the Swiss cantonal model. 'The Swiss constitution says that the cantons are sovereign within the limits of the constitution. At the same time there can be no doubt that Switzerland is a single sovereign member of the international community and that a United Cyprus Republic would be too. Furthermore, the plan explicitly says that the constituent states shall sovereignly exercise all powers not vested in the federal government.'

But Denktash dismissed de Soto's ingenuity, much like he did the 'virgin birth'. 'Sovereignly,' he says, spitting out the word with disdain. 'It was another little game they played in order to pay lip-service to our demand to be one of the two sovereign peoples in Cyprus. Have you ever found it in any legal text? A word that means you are not sovereign, but you use your rights sovereignly? We said what is this "sovereignly"? Why do you create new words?'

He refuses to admit that de Soto was trying his best to accommodate him. 'If it means what I mean, what I want it to mean, then why not put the correct word there?' Because as de Soto had explained, *ad nauseum*, as had his predecessors of the previous three decades, he simply could not.

Papadopoulos in, Clerides out

Less than a month after unveiling the first draft of his proposed solution for Cyprus, de Soto lost the key incentive which, it had been hoped, would drive the mediation towards a successful conclusion. At an EU summit in Copenhagen in December 2002 it was decided that even if there were no agreement on reunification, the internationally recognized Greek Cypriot part of Cyprus could join the EU on 1 May 2004. This followed a threat by Greece to veto the accession of nine other new members on the same date if this wasn't accepted. With EU membership assured, the balance of power at the negotiating table tipped dramatically in favour of the Greek Cypriots. In chess terms, de Soto describes this turn of events as tantamount to the Turkish Cypriots 'losing their queen'.

Did President Clerides immediately have the sense that with the Copenhagen decision they had the upper hand? 'Oh yes,' he says without hesitation. But what he had suddenly gained at the negotiating table he was rapidly losing in the Presidential Palace. Two months later, in February 2003, he was unexpectedly booted out by a discontented Greek Cypriot electorate in the first round of presidential elections. The people felt he was prepared to give too much away at the negotiating table, and that he had obsessed on getting a solution to the Cyprus problem at the expense of other all other issues. His successor at the Presidential Palace in Nicosia, and at the UN's negotiating table, was Tassos Papadopoulos.

Papadopoulos had benefited from a split in the vote. Clerides' had promised his right-hand man in the mediation, the Attorney General Alecos Markides, that he would stand aside for him in this election. When he changed his mind, saying it was his 'historic duty' to remain in office just 16 more months to see his country reunited by 1 May 2004, Markides left to form his own party. Papadopoulos, traditionally known as a hard-liner, reaped the benefits.

Also an old Cypriot political hand, Papadopoulos took office keen to play down the reputation his DIKO party had for its tough approach to reconciliation. In the election he had sent a reassuring message to the UN when he said he 'wanted' to take a united Cyprus into Europe. Although he did stress he was ready to negotiate 'a better settlement' first.

Papadopoulos' election, says de Soto, was a fatal blow to the Turkish Cypriots' bargaining position. 'With Papadopoulos in power they probably lost their rooks, and bishops and knights as well.' But it wasn't just a question of what the Turkish Cypriots lost; Papadopoulos' election was to prove a blow for the whole process. 'Everything changed when Papadopoulos was elected,' says de Soto, who admits he did not see it at the time.

The Hague meeting, March 2003

A month after Papadopoulos came to power, the UN, having put a solution on the table, sought to conclude the mediation process. All that was left to do was to get the leaders to agree to put the plan to a referendum. The meeting at which they would do this eventually took place on 10 March 2003 in The Hague.

A few weeks prior to this, Kofi Annan flew to Cyprus to cajole the new President Papadopoulos and Rauf Denktash into agreeing to this. But, according to Denktash, the arrival of the Secretary General was premature. 'I told Kofi Annan: "The visions are as far apart as they were in 1963 and we have not yet reached an agreement."'

This was despite de Soto previously explaining to Denktash: 'You are not being asked to agree to this plan. The only thing you are being asked is to allow the people to have their say.' De Soto puts on a voice of great self-importance as he puffs himself up to relate Denktash's reply, which was: 'I cannot take a decision like that on my own. I would have to call a referendum to ask the people whether or not they would agree to allow me to do that.'

Denktash would not be allowed to forget what he had said. When he tried to block the process moving forward, Kofi Annan, having been told of this response, was then able to say to him: 'I understand Mr Denktash, you are prepared to allow it to go to referendum.'

'By then,' says de Soto, 'Denktash realized he had set a trap for himself and he was already trying to wriggle out of it. So he said to the Secretary General: "Mr Secretary General, you know what my answer to that is ..." And the Secretary General cut in: "Mr Denktash, I don't want to hear your answer now, I want to hear it in The Hague ..." '

'No-ooo-ooo,' De Soto's face turns red as he recalls how Denktash's bellowed response reverberated around the Palais de Justice; the loudest 'no' he had ever heard delivered at the negotiating table. The Hague meeting had slipped from 10 March into 11 March as the UN team kept the two sides up all night in a 20-hour marathon as they tried in vain to persuade Denktash to let the plan go to referendum. With Denktash's 'no', which had been accompanied by a carefully calculated 'yes' from Papado-poulos, de Soto's mediation attempt came to a sudden end.

The international community was furious with Denktash. With his 'no', as David Hannay told him, he had 'pulled the plug' on the whole process. Denktash complains that he took all the blame and that Papadopoulos would have said 'no' himself if he hadn't said it for him. 'The Greek Cypriots said they agreed with the plan, and thought it excellent. They were playing the game they always played. The game they played until the end.'

New York, February 2004

At the annual gathering of world leaders in the lush Swiss ski resort of Davos in January 2004, the pro-EU Turkish Prime Minister Recep Erdogan raised the possibility of launching one final mediation attempt before half of the island was swallowed into the EU on 1 May. By now, it was almost a year since the process had been abandoned. Erdogan told Kofi Annan that Turkey had had a change of heart on the UN's Cyprus mediation. Turkey would now support the UN plan, and would accept the Secretary General having the final word on any aspect of it which the parties failed to agree on, before it was put to referendum. This significant policy shift from Turkey followed elections in the north of Cyprus which had sidelined Denktash in future talks. His party had lost, and a new prime minister, the moderate Mehmet Ali Talat, was now heading a pro-European, pro-UN plan coalition.

With these hopeful shifts in the political landscape, the talks were on again. So the plan was dragged back from near burial in UN archives and de Soto was recalled to Europe from the wilderness of the Western Sahara desert, where he had been sent following the collapse in The Hague. And an invitation was issued to the parties to resume talks in New York in February.

But it wasn't any old invitation. It was an invitation designed to push the process forward before it had even been resumed. In perhaps the most arch of all the word-traps which de Soto set along the way, was the rider on which the letter ended: 'By accepting my invitation to come to New York,' the Secretary General said, 'I take it you accept these conditions.' The conditions were that the Secretary General would have the final word on any aspect of the plan which the parties could not agree on, before it was put to a referendum. They were the same ones that Erdogan had just told the Secretary General he accepted, that the Security Council had endorsed – and that Papadopoulos had agreed to in The Hague, although he had only done this because he knew that Denktash would reject them. At this point, de Soto had skilfully exploited the reluctance of either side to be blamed for stalling the process. Both parties accepted the invitation to New York, but neither of them happily. Tassos Tzionis, who was then an advisor to President Papadopoulos and a member of his negotiating team, says it was tantamount to 'blackmail'.

Denktash was still participating in the process at this time, although he was now squashed between a Turkish government and a Turkish Cypriot government which were both in favour of the UN plan. Because he was now following the party line, not leading it, he arrived in New York to be given instructions from Ankara which said the 'negotiations must not break up in New York'. He claims he was surprised at having his capacity to block progress in the talks curtailed. 'Had I known that these were the instructions of Turkey, I would not have gone.'

In the opening meeting in Kofi Annan's office on the 38th floor, Annan outlined the conditions once more for reopening the negotiation. Denktash recalls that Papadopoulos responded immediately by saying: 'I do not agree with this.' In a move which called the UN's bluff, Denktash said simply: 'I agree with Papadopoulos.' With this the Secretary General closed the meeting, saying if they had not changed their minds by the morning the process would once more break up.

Since both parties had refused to accept the Secretary General's conditions, Papadopoulos' team were so confident that the game was now over that they sent their luggage to the airport ahead of their pending departure. But they would not escape so easily.

When Denktash walked out of the Secretary General's office, he had been accosted by a posse of American, British and Turkish diplomats. 'They were all saying: "How dare I agree with Papadopoulos". And I said: "Just a minute, isn't the purpose of the talks to agree with Papadopoulos?"' And Denktash breaks into a fit of delightful wheezy giggles.

But then Denktash remembered he had been instructed not to allow the talks to break up in New York. So the next day he backtracked, and proposed that before the UN 'fill in the gaps' on the plan, the two backers – Greece and Turkey – could help try and settle things first. There was nothing original in this: the Secretary General had already suggested that Greece and Turkey should be part of the final process. But Denktash's sudden show of enthusiasm for keeping the process going was enough to stymie Papadopoulos.

On hearing Denktash's proposal, 'Papadopoulos gasped and said I need a couple of minutes to consider this,' remembers de Soto. They were in unchartered waters. The roles were reversed. Denktash, albeit unwillingly, was now the one saying 'yes' and Papadopoulos was saying 'no'.

'At this point Papadopoulos, like Denktash, was committed to a process from which it would be very difficult to extricate himself,' says de Soto. De Soto and his team kept the pressure on them with back-to-back meetings which went on until around 2.30am. During this time Papadopoulos questioned whether or not the UN's tactics were 'legal' and Denktash complained of being starved into submission.

By 3.30am de Soto had finalized the agreement outlining conditions for restarting the talks and sent it to the Secretary General's residence. Shortly after 7am Kofi Annan gave it his clearance. An hour later the two parties, as well as Greece and Turkey, had a copy of the final conditions on which talks would resume. They were each instructed that no further negotiation was possible and that they must telephone de Soto by 10am that morning to say if they accepted these conditions. If they didn't call it would be taken as a rejection.

Despite the pressure, Papadopoulos had left the UN building in the early hours still refusing to agree to the conditions. It was becoming increasingly obvious to all concerned that he was prepared to sabotage the process so he could renegotiate from a position of omnipotence as an EU member after 1 May. The diplomatic community pulled together to let him know this was not on. So, in the early hours of 13 February, he got calls from ten different European heads of state and government saying simply: 'You had better accept the Secretary General's conditions.' Pressure from his future EU peers worked. Papadopoulos, albeit reluctantly, conceded. By 10am all four parties had phoned de Soto, accepting the terms on which talks would recommence.

And so the next few weeks were mapped out. There would be more talks in Nicosia, before a final week in the Swiss resort of Burgenstock. After that, the UN team would 'fill in the gaps' before putting the plan to a referendum a week before Cyprus – at least the southern part of it – became an EU member.

De Soto, who takes so such pleasure in the fine art of diplomacy, remembers the shenanigans of the New York meeting as 'wonderful, wonderful'. But wasn't there a danger of pushing these leaders through a process that they themselves, in the end, did not have to agree to? Wasn't it a high-risk strategy? 'Well, high risk?' responds de Soto turning serious. 'Did we have a choice? First I think we didn't have a choice. Second, the strategy was conceived to circumvent Denktash.'

And therein lay the problem. Denktash was no longer the one saying 'no'.

Preparing for the referendum

Perched at the end of the disused runway of Nicosia's derelict airport, de Soto's office had a commanding view of both sides of the city. Just below the building, the carcasses of planes, burnt out in fighting 30 years ago, still lay abandoned in this strip of Nicosian no-man's land. It was in these rooms, which had been hastily renovated at the start of the mediation, that de Soto's core team of five people worked drafting and endlessly redrafting the Annan plan, at times around the clock. On such occasions de Soto would leave his staff in the early hours to get a few hours sleep, before returning at dawn bringing croissants and coffee for everyone.

De Soto christened his handful of bright young international lawyers 'the plonkitects'. They were so-called because they were the architects of 'The Plonk', the name they fondly gave to the Annan plan because of the noise it made when dropped on the floor. As one of his staff says: 'He just couldn't let a pun go past.' De Soto's staff talk about their boss with affection. They say that although mostly much younger than him, he took their ideas seriously and enjoyed including them in the debate. And they all mention the fun of working in his office. On one occasion, when they'd just handed a draft to the parties and there was a lull, he got them all out of the office and on to the airport tarmac for a game of Frisbee.

After the parties from the New York meeting, the process intensified. There were now just weeks to go before the mediation process would end with the referendum. So the pressure was now on for de Soto to come up with a plan which would not only be accepted at referendum but one which could and would work in practice.

Mindful that many a peace agreement collapses at the stage of implementation, de Soto's team concentrated on producing a plan which was not just signable but workable. Whatever the leaders decided, should the plan be approved, the UN had to have a new country, in full working order, to present to the people the day after the referendum was held. Public competitions for a new flag and a new (wordless) national anthem had already been held but de Soto also had to come up with a federal government employing thousands of people. A new country, or even a 'new state of affairs' is a tall order by any standards. When you have only a matter of weeks to produce it, it is a serious challenge.

Several people on the mediation team had cut their teeth country-building in Bosnia implementing the 1995 Dayton peace agreement. The country created from this hurriedly put together peace deal was never thought through. It took several years before the lawyers, some of whom were now working on Cyprus, devised a way of implementing it. De Soto was determined that wouldn't happen again. So this time exceptional attention was paid to every last detail.

By the time the referendum took place, 6,181 people – including the cleaning ladies – were on standby to start work. Every aspect had been worked out, including their office space and email addresses. Every government office had a flag of the new United Cyprus Republic to fly on the first day of work.

Meanwhile, one of the undertakings that had been given to Papadopoulos, himself an exceptional lawyer, was that the plan would not go to referendum before the proposals for a federal government came equipped with a complete legal framework. This, too, had to be finished in time. So the tiny mediation team suddenly mushroomed from five to 50 people as experts on every subject were drafted in from around the world. These included secondees from other governments, the World Bank, the IMF, and the European Union. During these weeks de Soto's team, who were working round the clock, were picking up new staff everyday from the airport. One UN staff member remembers collecting a maritime legal expert who was not quite sure what he had come for, until an hour after landing he found himself chairing the committee charged with agreeing on laws of the sea.

These federal laws were agreed by these technical committees which were made up of several hundred Cypriot lawyers. When finally finished these laws, which formed the annexes of the Annan plan, totalled 9,000 pages. Unlike the 193-page plan which made a loud plonk when dropped, the annexes were undroppable.

At the final round of talks in the Swiss resort of Burgenstock, when the plan and its annexes were laid out, it took several tables to hold just a single draft. When the parties entered the room, people started helping themselves, assuming that everyone was expected to take a copy. It took Kofi Annan to stop them, explaining that the entire collection of paper laid out across the tables before them amounted to only a single copy of the plan. Everyone sheepishly put their section back.

It had taken such an enormous effort to get the unwieldy document printed in time for the Burgenstock meeting that it is understandable that even the Secretary General was protective of it. In trying to get just six copies printed for the Burgenstock meeting, the two most powerful printing presses on the island broke, and the UN team had to import larger, more powerful ones from Dubai. Finally, with customs officers having been given just 45 minutes' notice, rather than the usual 48 hours, the endless boxes containing the draft were taken under armed escort, sirens flashing, to the airport, loaded on to a plane, and from there headed for the final round of mediation in Burgenstock.

Burgenstock, March 2004
Nothing gets much closer to an image on a Swiss chocolate box than Burgenstock. Surrounded by snow-capped mountains with Lake Lucerne glistening below, the Burgenstock luxury hotel

complex is not a bad place to find yourself if you have a few days of intensive negotiation to get through. Or so you would think. Papadopoulos' negotiators describe their time there not as being locked in talks but locked up in a 'concentration camp'. After the talks, George Perdikis, a member of the Greek Cypriot team in Burgenstock, staged a photographic exhibition in Nicosia comparing the hotel complex to the Nazi-run concentration camp Dachau. Perdikis reflects the hostility among the Greek Cypriot team when he complains he was 'locked inside by United Nations staff' and his exhibition was meant to be 'a symbolic representation' of those 'manipulative' authorities who ran the Burgenstock talks.

Little progress had been made in the talks held in Nicosia during the previous six weeks. In Burgenstock, the parties had just seven days to finalize a plan. Although a further revision of the Annan plan was successively drafted in Burgenstock, this progress failed to move the mediation towards the UN's intended end-game.

At the outset there had been some hope. Denktash, who remained 'President' but whose party was now out of government, did not attend the talks. Moreover, he had given de Soto his assurance that the new Prime Minister Talat would have a free hand to negotiate. But even with Denktash out of the way, something went deeply wrong in Burgenstock. As de Soto observed, over the course of the mediation the Turkish Cypriots lost their queen, rooks, knights and bishops; Papadopoulos' wily team would no doubt claim, in Burgenstock de Soto lost his pawns.

The talks got off to a bumpy start with de Soto struggling to even get anyone to meet. He began by proposing an open meeting between the two parties in the presence of the Turkish and Greek Foreign Ministers, who were also present. The Greek Cypriots had said that they always wanted the chance to negotiate directly with Turkey. Before coming to Burgenstock de Soto had told Papadopoulos: 'Well, this is your dream opportunity.' But when offered the chance to sit face to face with the power behind Denktash's cardboard throne, Papadopoulos refused. 'Papadopoulos would not hear of it, he would not hear of it,' says de Soto, shaking his head still in disbelief. De Soto then suggested that just the Greek Cypriots and Turkish Cypriots met but the Turks said no. 'They had come to be fully involved in the process.'

Exasperated by this stage, de Soto decided to just get the lot of them around the dinner table. One of the invitees was not that enthusiastic. 'Papadopoulos did not want this, he only accepted after everybody else had done so,' de Soto says. But eventually they were all there at a private dinner, face to face, the Foreign Ministers of Turkey and Greece and the two Cypriot leaders. 'Had I known then that no quadripartite meeting had taken place in thirty years, I might not have been so bold,' says de Soto wryly.

But it worked. 'It was a great success. It was convivial and everybody was delighted that night. And they were all talking to each other. And that's what it was all about! That's what it was all about!' says de Soto, sounding like a frustrated conductor who has finally got his orchestra to play a tune. 'I had always had these dreams that one day all these core issues would be hammered out between two heavy smokers, in one knock-down, drag-out negotiation. That's what I wanted. That was the whole purpose of it.'

At the end of the meal everyone (except Papadopoulos) asked to do it again. That was Tuesday, 21 March. And de Soto suggested the following Friday night. Papadopoulos could not commit. He was not only not playing ball at Burgenstock, he went so far as to play hooky. In the middle of the talks Papadopoulos left. He had a meeting with the EU in Brussels. 'What can have been more important than this?' says de Soto, still incredulous at his audacity. 'It was the future of his country he was talking about.' De Soto tried to see him the night before he left but the President had 'other engagements'.

On that Friday night, having returned from Brussels, he sent de Soto a message that he was 'too tired' to attend the dinner, and so a Saturday lunch was organized instead. Time for the negotiations was nearly at an end. With Papadopoulos seated at his right and Talat on his left, de Soto leaned across to Papadopoulos and said quietly: 'I need to see you, Your Excellency. I need to see you today, this afternoon.'

And Papadopoulos told him he couldn't, he was busy, and he listed the people he had appointments with that afternoon.

'I can speak to every single one of those people and I assure you they will yield their time,' de Soto broke in.

'No, no, no,' replied Papadopoulos. 'Please don't.'

De Soto and Papadopoulos

What does de Soto attribute Papadopoulos' behaviour to? Usually de Soto responds to the infuriating behaviour of the negotiators in Cyprus with fond amusement, but this time he just sighs. 'I don't know. It is difficult to ascribe motive in this business.'

De Soto went to great lengths to get to the heart of his negotiators' needs. He once passed an hour chatting to Denktash in his swimming pool over the meaning of sovereignty. He showed interest in his enthusiasm for photography, and he listened as Denktash played him excerpts from his record collection of bird song. He regularly took tea in Clerides' drawing room, and more than once spent the day sailing with him on his yacht. With Papadopoulos things were very different. He gave de Soto no chance to let him form any kind of personal relationship. He evidently found sitting next to the touch-too-erudite de Soto, even at an official dinner, a fate to be avoided where possible. Even unscheduled chats were never on the agenda.

Without a text or an agenda in front of him, Papadopoulos, who was known in the negotiation for his focus on legal detail, not political vision, was simply not comfortable in his company. He admitted as much to de Soto himself in their first round of negotiation. De Soto says after the official meeting he suggested that he and Papadopoulos moved to a smaller room for a chat. He wanted to get to know his new interlocutor better, get to understand his point of view. 'So I went over the issues, and I tried to probe him to see where he was coming from. But he was deeply unhappy with this. And he said: "What are we doing here, Mr de Soto? Please explain to me what we are doing here. From now on, whenever I have meetings I'd like them to be scheduled in advance and know what the agenda is and know exactly what we will discuss." '

De Soto reflects for a moment. 'I don't know what he was telling me with that, but it already looked pretty bad at that point because he did not give the impression that he was accepting "the game". He wasn't prepared to play by the rules nor understand the etiquette.' As it later became clear, Papadopoulos had his own game to play. And replacing Clerides as Denktash's dancing partner in de Soto's carefully staged diplomatic waltz was never part of it.

In the 1950s Papadopoulos had belonged to extreme nationalist movements which sought to create a Greek-only Cyprus united with mainland Greece. Even though he had tried to hide his true political intentions under his electoral pledge to 'take a united Cyprus into the European Union', did de Soto's heart sink when he won the election? 'No, because I wasn't ready to accept the conventional wisdom then, which is that he was a hopeless rejectionist.' And Papadopoulos remains an enigma to him. 'To this day I still don't really know what he actually is.'

Redrafting in Burgenstock

Despite the tense atmosphere at the top political level, the negotiating teams worked throughout the week and the meeting in Burgenstock broke up with the Annan plan having been redrafted. Soon after, de Soto's team completed the fifth and final version, in which, as agreed, they 'filled in the gaps'. The Turkish Cypriots had negotiated enthusiastically during the Burgenstock talks. Talat says they were making up for lost time because until then, Denktash had always refused to contribute to the plan. 'The Turkish Cypriot side only really began to engage properly in 2004 once we were in office. It was very late in the process but in

Burgenstock we worked very intensely and did manage to successfully influence Mr de Soto and his team.'

Papadopoulos' side, who had worked only reluctantly with the UN team, complain that the outcome of the redraft in Burgenstock favoured the Turkish Cypriots. But the UN team worked on the principle that the overall balance of the plan be preserved. So any changes they made in favour of the Turkish Cypriots were matched in some way by changes favouring the Greek Cypriot side. But the UN team complain that the Greek Cypriots didn't make their job easy as they refused to prioritize the changes they wanted. Instead they presented de Soto's staff with a 44-page document of their demands. One UN staffer says: 'It was like a never-ending, ever-expanding shopping list. We said repeatedly to Papadopoulos' aides: "We need to know which changes matter to you most. Please don't leave us to guess." But maybe that's the way they wanted it.'

The less acceptable the plan was, the easier it would be for them to justify rejecting it at the referendum. Already at this point, the real focus of Papadopoulos' team was not on getting the best plan they possibly could for their people, but on preparing them to reject it at the referendum. 'While we were holed up busy revising the plan in Burgenstock, we failed to notice that in Cyprus Papadopoulos' lot had already begun their "No" campaign back home in the media,' says one of the UN lawyers involved.

The 'No' campaign

The professionalism of the Greek Cypriot 'No' campaign to encourage people to reject the Annan plan at referendum was impressive. In the weeks leading up to the referendum the whole of the south seemed to be covered with the word 'oxi', the Greek word for no. It was posted on cars, t-shirts, sprayed on walls and enormous banners were hung from apartment blocks. Even the church was involved, with bishops telling their flock a 'Yes' vote would be a ticket to hell. The English-language *Cyprus Mail* was one of the few media outlets disturbed by the campaign's unsettling sleekness. 'It operates on all levels using journalists, media owners, priests, deputies, ministers, businessmen and TV sitcoms and resorting to a variety of methods, ranging from distortion to suppression of information and from scaremongering to the stirring of xenophobia.'

The campaign played upon the historical significance of the very word 'oxi', which in Greek does not only mean no, it means no to foreign interference. Oxi day, which is celebrated on 28 October each year – and nowhere less so than Cyprus – marks General Mataxas' refusal to let Mussolini's troops occupy Greece at the beginning of the Second World War. It was not clear to those running the mediation, until the billboards screaming 'oxi' were already plastered across the country, that the very word 'oxi' was itself a gift to the xenophobia of those opposing the Annan plan. 'Yes, we missed that one,' says de Soto sombrely.

Although a decision was taken early on that the UN should not be seen to actively support what was a much weaker 'Yes' campaign, the international community was involved in trying to explain the plan. A Norwegian non-governmental organization Peace Research Institute Oslo (PRIO) widely distributed summaries of the plan and printed them in newspapers on both sides of the Green Line. But with little impact in the south.

Greek Cypriot television channels were overwhelmingly hostile to the plan and proved central to the 'No' campaigners' effort. It started in Burgenstock, when TV news had portrayed the meeting as a shambles at which their leaders had been treated disgracefully. It was easy for the presidential spin doctors to get this version of events relayed back home: like many a president, Papadopoulos can lord it over the state media. It is no coincidence that as the referendum drew closer, TV interviews with de Soto, his deputy Didier Pfirter, and the EU commissioner Gunter Verheugen were all cancelled.

The mediation's backers: the role of the US and the UK

A common belief among Greek Cypriots, so sharply reflected in the 'No' campaign, is that their country is simply a pawn on the international chessboard. Any interest shown in the island by external powers, particularly the former colonial ruler Britain, or the previous one, Turkey, or Turkey's biggest backer the US, is met with suspicion. Hence, the fact the only two countries to constantly back de Soto's mediation were the US and the UK was not lost on the Greek Cypriot population.

Anti-British sentiments are common in the south of the island. The UK, which granted independence in 1960, still retains sovereignty over three per cent of Cyprus, land which it uses to maintain military bases. Although a colonial anachronism, Britain's continued ownership of a small part of Cyprus was never on the mediation agenda. Its military bases there are too strategically important, as they are used not just by the British, but also the Americans as listening stations to monitor activity in the Middle East.

For much of the mediation, the US and UK envoys, Tom Weston and David Hannay, were actively engaged on a daily basis. They were involved in brainstorming over strategy, and acted as the diplomatic eyes and ears, providing the necessary 'diplomatic clout' to keep the whole show moving along. They were around so much that the UN team referred to them as 'The Cousins', a phrase found in John Le Carré's novels to describe the relationship between MI6 and the CIA, although one wit in the UN team had another explanation for their nickname, saying: 'You can choose your friends but not your relatives.'

Their familiarity with the process riled Papadopoulos's team. 'After every meeting you would see their US and the UK embassy cars outside de Soto's office,' complains Tzionis, noting the absence of other Security Council members from these intimate chats, such as the French and the Russians.

De Soto does not accept this, saying he was 'always available' to see any ambassador. He saw the French Ambassador at least twice a week, and the Russians 'quite regularly'; and during the course of the mediation visited Paris as well as Moscow. But it was only really Weston or Hannay who actually followed the process intensely and took a significant interest in the details.

Perceptions in a sensitive mediation, however, can be as important as reality. It was not only Papadopoulos' administration who perceived a specific diplomatic agenda behind the involvement of the US and UK. Some in the EU did too. One EU diplomat says: 'The main long-term objective of the parties supporting the process was to get Turkey into the EU – which is not on everyone's EU agenda, by any means.' De Soto, who has an established reputation as an impartial promoter of UN values and ideals, says simply it certainly was 'no part' of his agenda. 'Obviously Hannay and Weston knew a lot more about what was going on than any of the others but they knew very well that we were in charge because the Secretary General had insisted on it early on. He had stressed that the UN had the mandate and there would be no subcontracting.'

A last-minute Security Council Resolution fails
But it was a symbiotic relationship. De Soto relied on the US and the UK to step in when things were rocky. And it was the US and the UK who sought to save the UN's process once the effectiveness of the 'No' campaign became alarmingly clear as the date for the referendum grew closer.

When Papadopoulos' coalition partner the Communist party, Akel, in a political volte-face indicated it might also support a 'No' vote, international efforts to prevent this went into overdrive. Akel commanded a much more significant proportion of the vote than Papadopoulos' DIKO party, and as a traditionally pro-reconciliation party it had been assumed it would support the plan. Its backing was deemed crucial if there was to be any chance of the referendum being approved. Akel said it had 'security concerns' about the plan: it did not trust that the Turkish Cypriots or the Turks would implement it. Pandering to these concerns, just days before the referendum was due to be held, the US and the UK produced a Security Council Resolution bolstering the role of the UN peace-keepers in verifying compliance with the plan.

But the pandering backfired. In a move which surprised many, Russia exercised its veto, and the Resolution failed. The official reason for this was that Russia thought it wrong to try and influence the outcome of the UN-led referendum. European diplomats say the Russians told them they did this because the Greek Cypriots asked them to. The Greek Cypriots say the Russians told them that it was nothing to do with them. It was because the newly appointed Foreign Minister, Sergei Lavrov, wanted to make a point to the US and the UK that they should not abuse their positions as permanent Security Members to push through their own regional agenda.

On 24 April 2004, the people of north and south Cyprus finally got their chance to decide on the Annan plan. In northern Cyprus, where there had been a hearty debate and where – crucially – EU membership was dependent on a 'Yes' vote, 65 per cent of people agreed to it. In the southern part, where EU membership was assured, and the debate had been dominated by the masterful campaign against the plan, 76 per cent said no. And with this result, the door banged shut on what had proved yet another futile effort to re-mend this broken country.

Why was the plan rejected?

Papadopoulos' supporters would argue that they were not solely to blame for the negative referendum outcome. While it now seems self-evident that Papadopoulos always intended to defy the international community and enter the EU with a divided island and the upper hand, Tzionis says that Papadopoulos' response was affected by the style of de Soto's mediation.

Tzionis argues that they were bullied in New York, humiliated and ignored in Burgenstock and essentially the pawns of a US/UK/Turkish alliance aimed at pushing Turkey more easily into the EU. Like all good spin, it contains a certain element of truth.

Enough to exploit an insular island mentality, which convinced the ordinary folk of southern Cyprus what they probably already suspected: that foreign interference in their island was not to be trusted.

The New York meeting in February 2004 had been a turning point in the mediation. For the Turkish Cypriots it marked the beginning of their proper participation. For the Greek Cypriots it was when they say they stopped trusting the process. Tzionis says he 'completely disagreed' with de Soto's tactics in New York. 'In the end he resorted to the use of an ultimatum because we did not agree. We were told: "You accept it or the Secretary General will leave and go on vacation, telling the world that you have refused."' A UN team member tells a rather different story: 'In New York, Mr Papadopoulos was asked to agree to little more than the conditions he had accepted a year before in The Hague. These conditions were not dreamt up to trap him at all. And he had told the Secretary General only a month earlier how very eager he was to solve the problem before Cyprus joined the EU. I think his bluff was called.'

De Soto is not unsympathetic to the hostility their tactics in New York aroused. 'Having been a negotiator myself, I am sure it must have been very unpleasant, invidious.' But he stresses they did have a choice. 'They could have said no. It would have been at a political cost. It was their decision whether or not they were prepared to pay that cost.'

Unlike the parties, argues de Soto, the UN did not have a choice. It was obliged to do whatever it could to make the mediation succeed. These measures had only been taken because time was running out; there were a matter of weeks before Cyprus entered the EU, the leverage would be lost, and the process over. 'The Secretary General at that stage needed certitude as to what the parties were allowing him, empowering him to do,' de Soto says.

But it wasn't Kofi Annan who felt this empowerment as much as Alvaro de Soto. That conditional invitation to New York in

February 2004 had transformed de Soto's role. He was no longer a mediator, but – as the Secretary General's representative – an arbitrator. As Prime Minister Talat says, in this last phase, de Soto's position significantly changed: 'Instead of trying to convince each other, both sides were trying to convince Mr de Soto and his team of their cause so that they would decide in their favour.'

De Soto is aware of this. 'We took it very, very, very far,' says de Soto, dropping each word like a pebble into water. 'This was the Secretary General of the United Nations. What we were doing was extremely intrusive.'

But having taken it this far, de Soto wonders if in fact the problem was that the UN didn't take it far enough. His methodology was designed to circumvent obstreperous political positions at the negotiating table (originally with Denktash in mind). And this was done quite transparently so that democratic principles might prevail and the people presented with a balanced solution at the referendum. 'Maybe we should have gone a bit further by insisting that if it involves a referendum the leadership should remain neutral, above politics. The President could have just explained the pros and cons and then said: "It is up to you, my people, to decide."'

But such impartiality was hardly Papadopoulos' style, although you can imagine Clerides might have been game. The loss of Clerides at the negotiating table is something which de Soto now accepts was an early warning that the Greek Cypriots would pose a problem when it came to the referendum. 'Many say that the Greek Cypriot presidential election of 2003 was the referendum. And the reason Clerides was thrown out was that people sensed that he might be preparing to compromise and Papadopoulos didn't want to compromise.'

And he used the 'No' campaign to make sure that the people didn't want compromise either. Polls show the way in which the No campaign had distorted the understanding of the plan. People said they rejected the plan because they didn't like the fact not every single Greek Cypriot refugee could return home and that the majority who could would have to wait several years before doing so. The plan actually allowed for the majority of refugees to return, and because of a huge territory swap in the Greek Cypriot's favour, most of those returnees would be under a Greek Cypriot Administration. They also didn't like that Turkish troops would remain on the island 'indefinitely'. This wasn't as radical as it sounded. The final version of the plan was simply a reiteration of the agreement made at independence in 1960 which allowed 650 Turkish troops and 950 Greek troops to be permanently based on the island. They also didn't like it that many of the Turkish settlers would be allowed to stay. The plan actually made provision for a good portion of the Turkish settlers to return to Turkey, and it strictly controlled further Turkish immigration. Ironically, it was not the Greek Cypriots who would have had the most to give up. The largest sacrifice in the plan would have been made by the Turkish Cypriots: in order to allow the Greek Cypriots to reclaim their properties a third of them would have to move from their homes.

Details of the plan apart, de Soto thinks that the Greek Cypriots never really got their heads round the concept of equating a political minority, who made up 18 per cent of the population, with holding equal political rights. He questions whether to this day 'they accept the basic elements of a federal solution which are political equality and sharing of power with one's political equal'.

But there's much evidence to suggest the motivating reasons for rejection were far less intellectual; indeed that they had more to do with the effectiveness of the 'No' campaign than a rejection of the actual plan, which was clearly poorly understood.

The 'No' campaign was successful because all the talk of 'security concerns' had made people feel afraid. In the run up to the Greek Cypriot referendum, 80 per cent of people were saying they would vote no. At the same time, 70 per cent were admitting they did not understand the plan. When they left the polling stations 70 per cent said the reason they had voted no was 'security'. They did not 'trust the Turks' to implement the plan. They feared that Turkish troops would not stick to the agreement to withdraw from the island. Moreover, they feared that Turkey as a guarantor power might one day reinvade. For all of those in the international community hearing this, the thought that Turkey, the nation most desperate to enter the EU, would scupper its chances by invading an EU neighbour was patently absurd. But the people in the south hadn't heard this loudly enough because the international community had, on repeated occasions, not been allowed to speak.

Back in Cyprus, Clerides, whose last political act was to put his job on the line for the reunification of his country, is sanguine about the failure of de Soto's gut-busting attempt to solve the island's 'issue'. How long does he think it will take for his country to be reunited? 'Oh a very long time,' he says serenely. He takes a sip of tea from his bone china cup. 'Anyhow, why cry over split milk?' And he chuckles, the hearty chuckle of man who has seen off many a mediator, and who knows only too well that one day another one will be sent.

Postscript

Despite the failure of the plan, Cyprus did not quite prove to uphold its reputation as a mediator's graveyard as far a de Soto was concerned. His Cypriot mediation helped bolster his reputation as a mediator who survives the really tough jobs. He was rewarded for his efforts when a year after the referendum the Secretary General sent him to try and crack the uncrackable nut of Middle East peace. In May 2005 he moved to Jerusalem, taking up the post of Special Coordinator for the Middle East Peace Process and Personal Representative of the Secretary General to the Palestine Liberation Organization and the Palestinian Authority.

Selected sources

Books and reports

Report of the UN Secretary General on his mission of good offices in Cyprus, 1 April 2003.

Report of the UN Secretary General on his mission of good offices in Cyprus, 28 May 2004.

David Hannay, *Cyprus: the Search for a Solution*, published by IB Tauris, 2005.

Rebecca Byrant, *An Ironic Result in Cyprus*, published by *Middle East Report Online*, 12 May 2004.

Van Coufoudakis and Klearchos Kyriakides, *The Case Against the Annan Plan*, Lobby for Cyprus, 2004.

Caesar V. Mavratsas, *Politics, Social Memory and Identity in Greek Cyprus Since 1974*, www.cyprus-conflict.net

Rauf R Denktash, *The Cyprus Problem: What it is – How can it be solved?*, Cyrep, November 2004.

News sources

BBC News Online: News and Analysis.

Interview with Didier Pfirter in *KIBRIS*, posted on www.cyprus action.org/projects/loizides/pfirter.php

Helena Smith, 'Trying to paint out Cyprus's divisions', *Guardian*, 29 January 2002.

Jennie James, 'Will He or Won't He?', *Time Europe*, 23 February 2003.

Helena Smith, 'Cypriot leaders in last-ditch attempt at unification', *Guardian*, 3 October 2003.

'Coffee Shop', *Cyprus Mail*, 21 March 2004.

'Coffee Shop', *Cyprus Mail*, 29 March 2004.

'So close and yet so far', *Economist*, 22 April 2004.

Stephen Castle, 'Greek Cypriots look set to oppose UN plan', *Independent*, 23 April 2004.

US Secretary of State Colin Powell chatting to interim Afghani President Hamid Karzai and Lakhdar Brahimi in January 2002, during his first visit to Kabul following the signing of the Bonn Agreement the previous autumn which Brahimi had brokered. The Bonn peace conference was hurridly arranged just two weeks after the US bombing of the Taliban in the weeks following September 11, although Powell had wanted it held 'even quicker'. Brahimi later said of the agreement on which the current government is based: 'We've been criticized, quite rightly, that we did not get the whole package together in Bonn. It was simply impossible.'

The UN Secretary General, Kofi Annan, sitting next to his special advisor Lakhdar Brahimi during a meeting on Iraq at the UN New York headquarters in June 2004. Brahimi, who disagreed strongly with the US invasion of Iraq, 'reluctantly' agreed to be in charge of appointing the interim government in January 2004 after his staff say the US practically begged him to help. Despite being promised a 'free hand' to select candidates, his key choices were overridden at the last minute by those the Bush Administration preferred.

Alvaro de Soto shows the press the map of the proposed new Cyprus during the final round of talks in Burgenstock, Switzerland March 2004. During the week-long meeting to discuss the final revisions of the plan President Papadopoulos bemused diplomats present with his reluctance to participate. He even disappeared mid-week on a business trip to Brussels. 'What can have been more important than this?' wonders de Soto. 'It was the future of his country he was talking about.'

Alvaro de Soto chats to long-time Turkish Cypriot President Rauf Denktash in Nicosia, February 2004. Prime Minister Ali Mehmet Talat, who later replaced Denktash, can be seen between them. De Soto spent five years devising a plan for unifying Cyprus aimed at circumventing the intransigence of Denktash, only to find that it was the Greek Cypriots who actually rejected it under the hardline leadership of President Tassos Papadopoulos. This allowed the Greek Cypriots to enter the EU without their compatriots in the north, much to the fury of many in the international community on what was the 'biggest diplomatic effort the UN has ever undertaken, on any issue'.

Martin Griffiths sits between Chief negotiator for Indonesian Government, Sastrohandoyo Wiryono (L), and Chief negotiator Zaini Abdullah (R) of the rebel Free Aceh Movement, during the signing of a cessation of hostilities agreement at the Centre for Humanitarian Dialogue in Geneva in December 2002. Moments before the signing, the two sides pulled every reference to human rights from the agreement. Knowing that if the agreement was not signed, the Indonesian army would carry out a brutal military crack the following morning, Griffiths let the signing go ahead.

Colin Powell holds a private meeting with Sudanese Vice President Ali Osman Mohamed Taha and South Sudan rebel leader John Garang the day before the final signing of the peace deal on south Sudan in January 2005. General Sumbeiywo, pictured sitting in between the two principles, was often at loggerheads with the US over its approach to the mediation although he valued the support the process was personally given by Colin Powell.

Vidar Helgesen smiles as Chief Government Negotiator GL Peiris shakes hands with his Tamil Tiger counterpart Anton Balasingham, after the second round of peace talks in Nakhon Pathom Thailand, November 2002 which ended with a breakthrough on power sharing arrangements. Over the course of six rounds of talks, the two sides seemed to be on track to getting a negotiated settlement to a conflict in which 60,000 people have been killed.

President Kumaratunga, Vidar Helgesen and Erik Solheim in April 2002, shortly after the President had accused the Norwegians of exceeding their mandate in overseeing the signing of a ceasefire agreement between the Tamil Tiger rebels Kumaratunga's political rival Prime Minister Wickremesinghe. A year later the Tigers withdrew from the peace process. But just as they seemed ready to return to the table, the stalled process sunk into deeper crisis when Kumaratugna launched a 'constitutional coup' against her own government. She said so she did so because she feared they would give too much away to the rebels.

3 The Professional Maverick

Martin Griffiths
Aceh, Indonesia

Born in 1951, Martin Griffiths began his career working for UNICEF in Sri Lanka. He then trained as a barrister before joining the British diplomatic service. Following this, he moved to the Save the Children Fund, and then became Chief Executive of ActionAid. He joined the United Nations again in 1994, serving in Geneva, New York, the Great Lakes region, and finally in the Balkans where he helped establish the UN Mission in Kosovo. In New York and Geneva he worked in the UN Secretariat's humanitarian office, latterly as Deputy to the Emergency Relief Coordinator. He is the founding Director of the Centre for Humanitarian Dialogue in Geneva, which has been in existence since 1999.

On the night of Sunday, 8 December 2002, the Indonesian Government and the rebel Free Aceh Movement, known by its Indonesian acronym, GAM (Gerkan Aceh Medeka) were in the final frantic hours of deal-making. To Martin Griffiths, the mediator in charge of the process, it seemed that things were on track. The historic agreement between the two sides would be signed the following morning. Then one of the last-minute changes was presented to Griffiths, not as a proposal, but a *fait accompli*. And it was more than minor tweaking of the text. Both sides had pulled every reference to human rights from the final agreement.

Griffiths hesitated. Should he now scrap three years of torturous negotiations for the sake of these principles which the parties themselves had readily cast aside? 'If I had been working as a UN negotiator I would have had to,' he says. But he wasn't. As the director of the Centre for Humanitarian Dialogue (the HD Centre) he had been working in a private capacity. And unlike his UN or bilateral counterparts, who are constrained by both their bosses and international standards, he had no one to answer to but himself. So he had a choice; albeit an uncomfortable one.

Then his mobile phone rang. Skip Boyce, the American Ambassador to Indonesia had just been told by the Indonesians their army was amassed along the border of Aceh, ready to invade on Monday morning should the rebels fail to sign. And, Boyce added, US intelligence confirmed this. Griffiths laughs in slight disbelief at the profoundness of his own responsibility, as he recalls how Boyce ended the conversation saying: 'I am not telling you what you should do, Martin, I just thought you should know. I'm just leaving it with you.'

So Griffiths had to choose between upholding human rights on paper and protecting the human rights of the Acehnese the following morning. He let the deal go ahead and the next day the diplomatic great and good packed into the HD Centre's headquarters to watch the signing in front of an excited Geneva press corps.

Initially, the ceasefire more or less held and the Acehnese were granted a few months' reprieve from daily violence and insecurity. Then in May 2003, after weeks of deterioration, the Indonesian government declared martial law and carried out the military operation they had been planning five months earlier. Given that the agreement collapsed anyway, in the absence of human rights provisions would it have been better to stop the signing going ahead?

'I don't know, I don't know,' Griffiths says. 'We had really good language on human rights, it was excellent stuff they pulled out,' he adds, still sounding rather irked by the experience.

Griffiths and the HD Centre came under heavy criticism for the decision to go ahead with an agreement which did not, in the words of Human Rights Watch (HRW), 'even contain the term "human rights"'. Brad Adams, Asia Division Director at HRW warned at the time: 'The agreement won't stick without will on both sides to protect human rights and civilian lives.'

On reflection Griffiths accepts the criticism and the need, in legal speak, for a 'normative framework', which means conforming to international legal standards. 'I think in hindsight we should have put our foot down. In the event of another agreement we would.'

The private mediator

But in breaking the rules, as Griffiths did, he was also breaking new ground in peace mediation. Griffiths achieved what was seen in the mediation industry as an undoable deal. Like many a government with rebels on its hands, the Indonesians had always refused to allow outsiders to interfere in what it considered a domestic matter. Furthermore, it did not want the rebels to receive international recognition through a high-profile mediation. This was exactly what the GAM was after. The HD Centre is an organization closely linked to the diplomatic community, the UN and even the Red Cross, and so the GAM saw this mediation as a real opportunity to earn themselves a proper international profile. But Griffiths was a private mediator, representing a little-known organization, and so the HD Centre was also acceptable to the government.

Having an outfit like the HD Centre mediate, doesn't just suit touchy governments and rebels, it is very convenient for the international diplomatic community which, constrained by its own etiquette, likes to avoid getting its hands soiled by messy internal conflicts. Since he helped establish the HD Centre in 1999, Griffiths and his crew have met with some of the world's least palatable characters from the Sudan to Myanmar, from Uganda to Nepal.

Griffith's unconventional approach to peace has given him a controversial reputation in some quarters, particularly among some of the more strait-laced in the diplomatic community who see his Centre as breaking the diplomatic code of behaviour.

'They just went marching right in there,' says one mediator indignantly of their involvement in Darfur. What he meant was that they ended up as members of the international negotiating team, having got in via the rebels and not the government. 'Cowboys,' mutters one diplomat, disparaging a working approach that had involved HD Centre staff sleeping under the desert stars with the rebels.

It is not the first time Griffiths has heard this. 'The "cowboy" criticism is entirely lacking in an understanding of how we work,' says Griffiths. He argues that, unlike other mediators, because they operate outside the formal diplomatic framework they have to be 'fastidious' in examining the moral dilemmas, legal obligations and operational requirements of each situation. 'If you have to make up your own rules it tends to make you more cognizant of ethics and more disciplined.

'We operate with great care. We do not cross borders illegally, we always keep governments informed of, and generally in agreement with, our work. We're not cowboys at all. I spend most of my time examining pitfalls of what we're about to do, trying to work out what hindsight will later tell us we should have done.'

In the trade, Griffiths is termed a 'weak mediator', meaning that his institution cannot use power to push the parties into doing things. It has its advantages. Because they pose no threat, it means that parties may more readily accept them as a mediator in the first place, and in the course of that mediation let themselves get closer to them.

What they lack in actual political clout they make up for by ensuring they have access to it when necessary. As Griffiths admits readily, they could not operate without diplomatic support. 'We spend an enormous amount of time cultivating our relationships with the powerful players.' Throughout the Aceh mediation, for example, when Griffiths was not in Jakarta he was probably on a plane heading for Washington, London, Tokyo, Brussels or Oslo. Although in these exchanges their loyalty remained not with the diplomatic community but with the parties. 'It was always vitally important we never betrayed their trust,' says Griffiths, adding that the diplomatic community, especially the US, were incredibly supportive of the constraints under which they operated. Griffiths often says that the HD Centre would not have achieved what they did in Aceh without US support.

Their unconventional approach has meant that on several occasions the Centre has been quietly asked if they could give a kick-start to stagnant mediation processes *belonging* to other mediators. 'We spend a lot of time worrying about not interfering in other mediations, and frequently desist from following up an opportunity which might be seen as poaching. I'm not sure that diplomats display the same sensitivity.'

Perhaps there is just a little jealousy of the undeniable freedom that Griffiths and his team enjoy. Mediation without borders brings with it extraordinary opportunities for a peace mediator to delve into the underbelly of economic and political interests which drive war and push peace. Over the three years of the Aceh mediation Griffiths was asked to broker deals with oil giants, negotiate the Centre's way through a series of extortion and protection rackets, and had to stop one of the parties being declared official terrorists by his chief backers, the US.

The road to conflict in Aceh

The resource-rich province of Aceh has a history of resisting colonization. Centuries of fighting off the Dutch turned into decades of resistance to Indonesian rule after 1949, when the Netherlands granted Indonesia independence with Aceh thrown into the deal. Then, in 1971, oil and natural gas were discovered in Aceh. Suddenly, the province which was once one of many rebellious areas in a complex country made up of thousands of islands took on a greater significance. Oil and gas meant that Aceh filled up with foreign companies, who preferred to employ outsiders rather than locals to work in their production plants. In turn, these oil companies started filling Indonesia's central coffers with millions of dollars – dollars which the impoverished local population of over four million people barely saw.

From this resentment in 1976 the Free Aceh Movement was spawned, led by Hasan di Tiro, a descendent of the province's pre-colonial sultanate. And with the birth of GAM began a conflict in which over the following three decades more than 12,000 people – mostly civilians – would be killed. It was a dirty war, with dirty rules, characterized by arbitrary executions, kidnapping, torture and disappearances, and the torching of villages. While GAM was not guiltless in this grim list of activities, human rights groups repeatedly point to the Indonesian Army as being responsible for atrocious human rights abuses in its suppression of the rebellion.

For the first 20 years of the GAM's guerrilla resistance the Indonesian government, which during this time was under the heavy hand of President Suharto's military rule, did what it could to brutally repress the rebellion. Then, in the second half of the 1990s, Indonesia underwent some dramatic changes which forced the government into contemplating external mediation: in the wake of the 1998 Asia financial crisis, Suharto was ousted after more than 30 years in power, making way for a brief interlude of more reformist leadership firstly under Vice-President Habibi and then under the erratic presidency of Abudarraham Wahid. Then, in 1999, the former Portuguese colony of East Timor, under intense international pressure, was granted independence.

The independence of East Timor raised hopes among the Acehnese, and fear in the Indonesian establishment, that the international community would support Acehnese independence. And perhaps not just for Aceh. The possibility that East Timorese independence could mark the beginning of the break up of their nation along the lines of Yugoslavia and the Soviet Union was an alarming thought for Indonesia's nationalist establishment. And it was an important factor in driving the Indonesians to the negotiating table.

'There was a need in Jakarta for a ceasefire,' says Griffiths. 'It was seen by the main political parties as a solution to this problem which had not been solved militarily. Some saw it as good international politics – good for foreign investment; good for their relations with the US.' He says the Indonesian Foreign Minister Hassan Wirayuda once told him that 'Aceh was the hinge for creating stability in Indonesia. It will show these other areas of tension that peace can be made.' Despite this, the Indonesian political establishment remained hostile to the very thing they had come to negotiate. 'Like practically any government in this situation, the notion of independence in Aceh remained an anathema. But this meant there was little political room for manoeuvre which made getting a peace agreement so much more complicated.'

In 1999, the newly formed Henry Dunant Centre for Humanitarian Dialogue, as it was then known, had itself become involved in a peace bid for Aceh after sending a researcher to East Timor, which was then in the last violent throes of Indonesian rule. Finding there was nothing 'useful' that the Centre could contribute to the situation there, it was suggested to them by someone working in East Timor that they look at the situation in Aceh.

They did, and before long it was a question of getting the Indonesian government on board with the idea. Griffiths credits President Wahid with pushing the issue of talking peace in Aceh through his cabinet. Wahid now has a reputation for having run an erratic administration but Griffiths found him to be a thoughtful Islamic scholar who believed in the principle of engaging in dialogue. 'I asked him once, when we were alone together in the back of his car, why he chose us. He said he had had two heroes in his life: one was Florence Nightingale, the other was Henry Dunant.'

In a very clear show of support for the Centre which carried his hero's name, the Indonesian President came to its Geneva headquarters in January 2000 to make a speech in support of the peace process. The Centre had been in existence for just a few months and negotiations on Aceh were just getting off the ground. 'It was a big coup,' remembers Griffiths. 'He said I want to come here and show the world, particularly my cabinet, that he put his trust in the HD Centre. It was a political act.'

On paper Wahid looked like a promising candidate for a peace-deal in Aceh. He had a reputation as a religious and political moderate and had taken office on a ticket of reform. Soon after coming to power in October 1999, he had apologized for the vicious human rights abuses which had just taken place in the run up to independence in East Timor. Moreover, in response to pro-independence rallies in Aceh, he said he would support an autonomy referendum taking place in the province. 'I support a referendum as their right. If we do it in East Timor, why not in Aceh?' he told a press conference in Jakarta. But he stressed his government would first have to consult 'all parties'.

No consultation was necessary. On hearing this, politicians from across the spectrum of Indonesia's establishment responded angrily, not least General Wiranto, the former head of Indonesia's military and Wahid's Security Minister. Wiranto already had reason to be hostile towards the President, having been linked to many of the human rights abuses in East Timor for which Wahid had apologized.

Like many of Wahid's pledges, his support for a referendum was quickly swept under the political carpet. His physical frailness – he was almost blind and had suffered several strokes – reflected his political vulnerability. He was never secure enough to push such wild promises through. But in his own way, he did try. When he came to the HD Centre on that chilly January evening so early on in the process, diplomats present best remember the way he used his speech not to express polite support for the HD Centre's role as mediator but for letting it be known he intended to sack Wiranto. With his military-backed Vice-President Megawati Sukanoputri waiting edgily in the wings, this did nothing to secure his position back home in Jakarta.

Griffiths, the independent mediator

The HD Centre is not what you would expect. In any other country this elegant villa of balustraded staircases and high arched windows overlooking Lake Geneva in the middle of a public park would be a café, full of noisy ice-cream-covered children. But this is Geneva and in Geneva elegant villas in public parks get used for other purposes, such as peace.

Upstairs in the Centre in what once was the bedroom of a gentleman doctor, Martin Griffiths' office exudes the muted good taste of a Swiss designer: plum leather sofas; a well-worn Oriental rug; a computerless, paperless desk. He sits looking out beyond the roller-bladers, prams and dog walkers in the park below, across the lake. But he doesn't want to talk about peace, he wants to talk about kids. Like all good mediators, Griffiths starts on common ground. He knows we both have them. 'There's nothing like them, is there?' he says, his bright blue eyes narrowing in delight under a mop of silver hair.

He has had many incarnations before entering fatherhood in his late forties – diplomat, non-governmental organization (NGO) worker, UN boss, and now, peace mediator – but the pleasure of this one clearly still surprises him. 'I mean, everyone says it, but you only realize it when you have your own. It's just so wonderful.' This is not just small talk: bonding on a personal level is the bread and butter of his work as a mediator, as he later admits. 'It's all about, you know, you have a child, so do I. There is no more natural human bond than talking about your children.'

Griffiths is rather arty looking. The combination of his twinkly eyes and pale hair, the talking with his hands, and his deep melodious voice, give him an actorish air. He describes himself as Welsh, but sounds terribly English. And seems it, particularly when practising his batting stroke with a bottle of mineral water while musing on the pros and cons of sovereignty.

On this and many other topics Griffiths is a bit of a radical. Griffiths describes his default setting as 'definitely not statist', which means when it comes to mediating civil wars he does what he can to avoid mediations which depend on exploiting the natural advantage governments have over rebels at the negotiating table. For him, it matters that there is someone 'in the trade', as he calls it, who occupies this niche. 'I think it's important we represent a different moral view of the world. I don't consider myself an overly moral person. It's not that. It's just that governments aren't everything and are not always right.'

In taking this stance, he has challenged the widely accepted notion that mediation of insurgent groups is, in part, an exercise in containment and co-option. 'We try hard not to be biased towards power. There's a great deal of this about in mediation, as any mediator knows. Diplomats of powerful governments can be very patronizing in this respect – that's why they find themselves calling us "cowboys".'

Within the international establishment, not least the United Nations, he says rebels are treated with disdain. 'Of course, there has to be protocol to deal with the difference between an elected government and a non-elected rebel movement. For the UN, rebels are a bit like NGOs but only worse. And it's just plain wrong. We should remember that Nelson Mandela was one once.'

Such remarks suggest an idealist. But when asked if his professional heart comes from his many years at the bumpier end of humanitarianism, at Save the Children Fund and then as head of ActionAid, Griffiths is keen to stress his first real job was as a diplomat.

Although Griffiths accepts he has a reputation as a maverick, he is certainly more insider than rebel in the international diplomatic and humanitarian elite. His whole career has been woven in this world. He could not operate at the level he does without being securely plugged into both the UN, diplomatic and British establishments.

On the face of it, Griffiths could certainly still pass as a diplomat. He speaks in measured, well-formed sentences without changing tone even when expressing anger or bitterness. It is only the odd adjectival 'fucking' he occasionally lets slip, that suggests there is still a bit of the impulsive aid worker in him. He says he is motivated by 'anger at the establishment' and that what drives him is 'the humanitarian impulse ... to get something done so that a life is saved'. His Foreign Office background meant that he was unperturbed in taking this 'impulse' into the realm of top-level peace mediation, traditionally a preserve of gentlemen diplomats, not aid workers.

Griffiths argues that there is a moral imperative for peace mediation to be about more than a means of getting a document signed at the political level; it should also be an opportunity to get the parties to engage in the responsibility they have for the suffering of their people. 'We do see the Centre as a political project in a way. The humanitarian approach to mediation is particular: it sees mediation as a way of saving lives and not just as a path to a peace agreement.'

In 1999, just as the HD Centre was starting, he mapped out a new thesis entitled the 'New Prevention', in a speech which argued that the work of humanitarian and human rights organizations should be woven into the political peace-making process. 'The thinking behind the New Prevention came from the frustration at the limitation of humanitarian action. We wanted to make "humanitarianism" more relevant and more fundamental. It's a very common frustration among humanitarian workers. We've been lucky enough to get a chance to do something about it at the design level.

'Of course it's a challenge to the more pure definitions of humanitarianism but on the whole those organizations have been kind to us.'

Most may have been kind, but not all are comfortable with it. In 2002, the International Committee of the Red Cross (ICRC) asked the Centre to remove the name Henry Dunant from their title. Even though Griffiths had invoked the name of the founder of the Red Cross movement in his speech outlining his theory for the New Prevention, three years later his *modus operandi* had proved a touch too controversial for an organization whose second name is neutrality.

The Centre obliged, changing its title to the Centre for Humanitarian Dialogue; although the ICRC made an exception for the mediation in Aceh where the name was already in use.

Aceh's humanitarian pause

Until Aceh, Griffiths had never done a formal peace mediation. He had frequently negotiated humanitarian issues between warring parties, and he used this experience to get the two sides to start talking. But things got off to an awkward start when the GAM refused to enter talks. It was then that Griffiths put the ideas contained in the New Prevention to the test.

'They said they had a policy never to sit down with the Indonesian government. We had to overcome that – we did it speciously by saying they were not going to formally "sit down" with them, they were just going to talk about humanitarian issues.'

This led to the first breakthrough in the Aceh mediation with the signing of the Joint Understanding on a Humanitarian Pause in May 2000. This quasi-truce had both sides agreeing to 'reduce the violence' and improve security sufficiently to help deliver humanitarian aid to areas in need. As Kira Kay of Princeton University says, it was a means of doing one thing, while making it look like another: 'Framing the dialogue in humanitarian terms provided a face-saving cover for concessions by both parties, making compromises appear as ... noble acts, rather than strategic losses.'

Initially at least, the level of violence dropped. In the first six months of the Pause, 69 civilians and 14 members of the security forces were killed in Aceh compared to around 400 during the first four months of the year.

But even at this early hopeful stage in the negotiation process, differences in the meaning of the Humanitarian Pause were evident. The GAM presented it as 'halfway towards Aceh's freedom'; while the government remained publicly ambivalent about its own involvement in peace talks. At the last minute, the Foreign

Minister decided not to attend the signing because it was feared that his presence at the signing ceremony would imply recognition of the rebels. Even once agreed, the Humanitarian Pause was politically unpopular in Jakarta. It was widely attacked among the Indonesian political establishment, and the defence ministry complained it put the GAM's military wing on a footing with the TNI (the armed forces of Indonesia). For many in the military, the peace process was unnecessary. For them, the solution to the rebels in Aceh was simple: destroy the GAM.

The Pause may have reduced levels of violence but it did nothing to lessen the mistrust on both sides. The Indonesians accused the GAM of using the opportunity to tighten its control of the countryside and set up alternative governmental structures. The GAM, on the other hand, believed the army was using the protection of vital installations like the giant Exxon-Mobil plant in North Aceh to send in reinforcements. Throughout the process both sides used any lull in military activity to strengthen their positions on the ground. But what they may have gained in tactical manoeuvres they lost in confidence at the negotiating table.

In January 2001, talks in Geneva had made 'substantive' progress and the fragile Humanitarian Pause was renewed for a further month. In those talks they had agreed in principle that the conflict could only be resolved with a free and fair election, monitored by outsiders in which GAM could take a full part. When these conclusions arrived back in Jakarta they were shelved with almost immediate effect. Although Vice-President Megawati had seemed to support the continued process by meeting Griffiths at the Hilton in Geneva while there 'on other business' in January 2001, she had, by then, other plans for resolving the conflict. In what would become known as the NAD (Nanggroe Aceh Darussalem) law, Megawati was planning to present GAM with her own take-it-or-leave-it autonomy package. If they refused, military operations would be resumed.

Knowing that he must try and keep the momentum of the January talks going, in February 2001 Griffiths went to see

President Wahid in the Presidential Palace in Jakarta to persuade him to get the Humanitarian Pause reinstated. What he most remembers about that meeting was the state of the Presidential office. There was a bicycle propped up against the wall behind his desk which was piled high with classical music cassettes, and some dry-cleaning had been slung over a chair. 'Of course you realize he can't see this so it doesn't matter to him that his office is a shambles.'

The chaos of Wahid's office mirrored the state of his administration, which in the following months began to fall apart. During this time Wahid came under intense pressure from the Indonesian military to let them crack down on the spiralling violence in Aceh. In April, stopping short of a full state of emergency, he signed a decree ordering security forces to restore law and order. In July 2001 Wahid was impeached, accused of corruption and incompetence, allowing his deputy Megawati to come in and tidy up the Presidential office. And with her arrival as head of state, the Indonesian military re-established its influence in Jakarta.

Oiling the process

In March 2001, just weeks after the Humanitarian Pause formally ended, the American oil giant Exxon-Mobil suspended operations in Aceh because of increasing attacks by GAM on the company and its employees. In 1971 when oil and natural gas reserves were discovered in Aceh, Mobil, as it was then, had been one of the first foreign companies to set up operations. Thirty years later, the American giant was reportedly bringing in over $1 billion worth of revenues to the Indonesian government each year. So the pull-out was expensive for both Exxon and the government. Even though the Indonesians' enthusiasm for negotiating peace through the HD Centre was certainly on the wane at this point, it found it could nonetheless exploit Griffith's status as a private mediator to help broker the war. 'Once Exxon pulled out we noticed that the Indonesians became very keen for us to get a deal with GAM in order to protect the Exxon sites,' he says. 'And so we conveyed these messages about the need for ending attacks on the Exxon sites to the GAM.'

Griffiths defends their foray into the realm of Indonesia's business interests – something he admits neither the UN nor a bilateral mediator could have done – on the grounds that it was necessary to their own work. 'There is clearly a very direct relationship between economics and peace. While we had no interest in Exxon's operations, and no interest in Jakarta's income, we did have an interest in making sure these issues did not get in the way of our negotiations. We wanted to get things back on track.'

During these sub-negotiations, Exxon-Mobil refused to meet the Centre directly for talks, saying it was not appropriate for a 'contractor to the Indonesian government' to do so. But its role in the conflict and thus its importance to its resolution should not be underestimated: for the Indonesian Army, the TNI and the GAM it was a vital source of revenue.

The Indonesian Government does not provide all the revenues necessary to run its army; some estimates suggest it only provides 30 per cent of them. The army compensates for this dramatic shortfall, in part by providing private 'protection' to huge foreign companies like Exxon-Mobil working in unstable areas like Aceh. This is another reason why the Indonesian military was seen to have little interest in a successful peace process in Aceh.

AM, meanwhile, officially gets its money from 'contributions from the Acehnese people'. But its much more lucrative 'taxing' comes from extorting money from local and international contractors. Exxon-Mobil has admitted receiving extortion letters purportedly from the GAM although a company spokesman has been quoted as saying 'We have never knowingly paid money to GAM.'

By July 2001, the Indonesian government, feeling the pinch from the loss of revenues, demanded that Exxon-Mobil resume operations. If not, it said it would be expelled from the country and its assets taken over by Pertamina, the state-owned enterprise in which Exxon has a 35 per cent stake. Reluctantly, Exxon resumed operations on the condition that the Indonesian army resumed providing protection.

This wasn't the first time the HD Centre had acted as a go-between for the government, Exxon and GAM. 'In 2000, we had successfully mediated the GAM out of one of the Exxon installations they were occupying. We literally got the GAM to hand over the keys to the place which we then handed over to the American Embassy in Jakarta.' Griffiths says this hands-on approach simply helped them do 'useful things for peace in Aceh', although he admits 'perhaps we stretched things further than others would have done'.

Talks sink into deadlock

With Wahid in the final fumblings of his presidency, and an ongoing military crack-down taking place in the violent province, Griffiths somehow managed to get the two sides to sit down and talk in June 2001. Human rights groups estimate more than a thousand people had been killed in Aceh in the previous six months. Against this depressing backdrop, Griffiths remembers the talks as the occasion he watched the process he had spent so long nurturing, slipping away. 'It was an awful meeting and everything was breaking down.' It wasn't just the process that was on the verge of snapping, Griffiths was, too. During the meeting he had to stop himself from hitting the Indonesian Chief Negotiator, Hassan Wirayuda.

It was clear that Wirayuda had been instructed to make sure the talks made no progress. And so he was finding reasons to refuse to agree on an agenda. 'He was destroying the process. And he pulled some ridiculous procedural trick on me. And I raised my hand and I was literally about to hit him – the Chief Negotiator for the Indonesian government! And my deputy, Andrew Marshall, was sitting next to me and he said: "Don't do that!" So I let my hand hit the table instead. But he knew what I had been about to do.'

The moment exposed the extent to which mediation is often nothing more than role-play, and those involve know it. In the corridor afterwards, Griffiths said to Wirayuda: 'Thank God I didn't do that,' and Wirayuda laughed.

'It was a good moment,' says Griffiths. 'He obviously understood why I was so angry. It's through those kind of experiences that you bond.' Griffiths now talks of having a warm friendship with Wirayuda, who became Foreign Minister under Megawati. He says he was one of the people who kept him going through the long, barren months of mediation that followed.

Megawati in power

At first it seemed to Griffiths that Megawati becoming President in July 2001 might help the peace process. After the uncertainty of Wahid's reign, here was a woman who was in control. She appointed to key positions in her cabinet people who were already closely involved in – and generally supportive of – the process. These included Hassan Wirayuda, as Foreign Minister, and Susilo Bambang Yudhoyono, who later succeeded Megawati as President, as Security Minister. 'At least we had a government with a sense of purpose,' says Griffiths.

But it wasn't a common purpose. Megawati was still taking a unilateral approach to peace in Aceh. A few days after assuming office she approved a special autonomy law, known as the NAD law. On paper it looked like the government was making significant concessions to the GAM. Under the law the province was renamed Nanggroe Aceh Darussalem (NAD); its share of oil and gas revenues would increase from five per cent under Suharto to 70 per cent; and Aceh was allowed to implement Shari'a law. But the law, which was never, in fact, implemented, was riddled with problems: although it appeared the government was offering a real financial incentive, it was unclear if the oil and gas revenues refer to the total production in the province or simply part of it; many Acehnese saw the introduction of Shari'a law as being a deliberate ploy to politicize what was not essentially a religious conflict; the law said nothing about what might happen to Indonesia's large military presence in the province; nor did it remove the political elite dominated by the incumbent nationalist party Golkar.

Megawati's rise to power left the Centre mediation in limbo. What had already become a low-key process was suddenly halted in July in 2001 when police arrested six GAM negotiators in the hotel in Banda Aceh where talks were taking place. The reason for these arrests, the Indonesians said, was that an Achenese flag had been raised at a pro-independence rally held by the GAM.

Once more the HD Centre found itself weighing in to mediate not peace but the grim realities of the continuing war. Within a couple of weeks, Griffiths – with the help of the Americans behind the scenes – had negotiated their release. For Griffiths, subjugating his personal views of arrests like this, and neutrally brokering the uneven power relationship between the Indonesian government and the GAM, was vital in order to keep the process going. 'As a mediator, it must be a central preoccupation balancing your first duty which is to push the process forward with your normal views about people's rights. After all, what's wrong with raising a flag?'

As a go-between the Centre retained enough usefulness for the government not to completely abandon their mediation. But once in office, Megawati made sure the Centre's status was very clearly downgraded. 'I never met Megawati once she became President and I had met with Wahid all the time. That was obviously intentional,' says Griffiths. 'You need the attention of the head of state on such matters. It made life much more complicated.'

Peace in limbo
For the rest of the year the peace process hung in limbo. The GAM predictably rejected the NAD law. And the Indonesians' brutal crack-down continued.

During those fruitless six months of 2001, Martin Griffiths spent much of his life on a plane between Jakarta and the GAM leadership who were in exile in Stockholm. In all, during 2001, even though there were hardly any talks, he did the Jakarta–Stockholm trip 13 times. His personal assistant Judyta Wasowska describes how, in a very literal sense, he put himself at the beck and call of the parties. 'He would receive a call from the Indonesian Foreign Minister asking him to convey a message to the GAM. He would drop everything. And that afternoon he was on a plane to Jakarta where he would spend a few hours before heading off to Stockholm.'

The time he spent in taxis and the airport departure lounge gave him many hours to reflect on his new role as a message carrier. 'The really hard times for people in our position are the barren times like that when you start wondering if you are complicit in a fraudulent process. We are the perfect example of the "weak" mediator. We have no axe to grind. But as a weak mediator you have to be very careful not to be co-opted by the more powerful party.'

The Indonesian government did not shy from exploiting its position. 'Sometimes, I'd go to Jakarta for a meeting which then didn't take place. And I'd have gone half way round the world for nothing. Although it looks more tricky, it's actually much easier when you are moving and implementing. The dry times are definitely the worst. I think morale was very difficult then.'

The Griffiths approach

Griffiths says it was his job to act, when necessary, as a 'humble servant'. At this point in the process he had to do this if there was any hope of keeping the mediation afloat. 'We kept saying: "We are here as long as you want us." We said to all the parties: "We are your servants."'

But sometimes, even for someone of such dogged patience, it's a hard act to sustain. He talks of getting 'very, very irritated' by the way the parties exploited his self-confessed servility. 'It's exasperating when you've gone with what you think is a perfectly reasonable proposal and they simply refuse to consider it. And you think, God, who does believe in making peace here? It's not my people who are suffering. You just want to shake them because you just want the process to move on.'

These frustrations are part of the role of the mediator. 'You often feel that you are acting a lot. I was a diplomat a long time ago but this is more of an act. One feels it more. But it's not an insincere performance, it's a sincere one.' Griffiths was not alone in role-playing. The parties did it, too. To raise the stakes. To change the atmosphere. To wind each other up. And, when necessary, to wind Griffiths up too.

He remembers an occasion when the Indonesian Chief Negotiator Wiryono Sastrohandoyo infuriated him by accusing him of losing his neutrality. 'He said: "This piece of paper which you, Griffiths, have drafted, just shows your bias. You have no interest in this process, it is totally pro-GAM and you have insulted us by producing such a document."'

Wiryono had known exactly where to put in the knife. For Griffiths, to question his neutrality as mediator was to question his integrity. 'This casual slur, made as a throw-away line, hit me very hard. I was incandescent with rage. I don't get angry very often and it can be quite useful to step out of the role of the mild-mannered mediator. Step out of the room actually because I just could not take it.' Wiryono later apologized. 'It was a very authentic thing. I think getting through the performance to that emotional reality is deeply important.'

Griffiths does this himself with consummate skill. His colleagues talk about his capacity to break through the crusts of diplomatic and political pomp and bond with his fellow man. He is mercurial in conversation, never contradicting, never pontificating, presenting others' ideas with more certainty than his own, and never playing the all-knowing patriarch. After the pretensions and self-importance of so many in the diplomatic community, his unaffectedness and the fact he doesn't take himself, or anyone around him too seriously, is refreshing.

He is aware of this. He has, by his own admission, a handle on the vital art of charm. Asked what the key skills are in getting the parties to open up and start talking he says it is firstly trust. And secondly charm. 'The business about charm is manipulation,' he says *sotto voce*, before adding: 'You've got to be genuinely charming, haven't you? You've got to feel it.'

But underpinning the charm, he says, is the need to make a genuine relationship with the negotiators from each party. 'The familiarity of that personal relationship is beyond measure in this business. I can't think of a professional process where a deep personal sympathy is more important. They are putting the future of their people in your hands. They are making terribly difficult decisions. And so they have to know you, and they've got to trust you.'

But are these relationships genuine, since as a mediator, you want something from them? 'These relationships have an objective. I am not just here to be their friend. But I don't actually find this to be a contradiction. Perhaps I am too far in it to see it. I haven't found this to be a great moral dilemma. I can't think of an instance where I've been involved in something which I am seeking to push which I've thought is wrong.'

And what does he do when his renowned charm or the ties of friendship fail to work? 'Bluff,' he says, without a moment's hesitation. But he adds: 'Bluff is very important, but it only works once out of 25 times, if you are lucky. More than that I think is trust.'

Enter three wisemen

As 2001 wore on, months of message-carrying showed no signs of bearing fruit. Asked if he thought at that time if he would succeed in getting an agreement signed, Griffiths reflects for a moment, almost says no, and then changes the subject.

In that summer, the mediation's most important backers, the US, were also concerned about the lack of progress. And so they came up with the idea of appointing high-profile envoys to the process in a bid to get it going again. 'It wasn't our idea,' says Griffiths. 'The State Department thought we needed leverage, that we had been kicked around too much.' With slightly bizarre symbolism, for a conflict in a predominantly Muslim nation, these envoys would be known as the 'Wisemen' and there would, in principle, be three of them: General Anthony Zinni of the US, Dr Surin Pitsuwan of Thailand and Ambassador Budimir Loncar of the former Yugoslavia, although later they were joined by a senior official from Sweden, Bengt Save-Soderburgh.

Because of the sensitivities of the US being so directly involved in the process, publicly the Centre took credit for the Americans' Wisemen initiative. 'We were in a difficult moral position about whether this should come out because it seemed better that it appeared to the outside world that it was our idea. So we decided not to tell the world that it wasn't our idea. But we would tell the parties. Because we should not lie to the parties, that was our main thing.'

Megawati's government needed some convincing. 'The Indonesians took a long time to accept the idea. Finally they did, as long it was quite clear that they were our advisors, and we were not their advisors.'

The war on terror

The context in which the negotiations were taking place changed dramatically with the events of 9/11. Relations between the US and Indonesia evolved significantly over the following year, as Bush's war on terror got under way. And these changes had a knock on effect on the search for peace in Aceh – not all of them positive.

In the spring of 2002, largely driven by the war on terror, the US started seeking to re-establish military ties with Indonesia. These had been severed following the brutal military crack-down in East Timor in 1999. Much of the multi-million dollar package on offer was to be used in the support of domestic counter-terrorist efforts. Many in the Indonesian establishment were ambivalent about such an offer: Bush's war on terror, with its skewed focus on all things Islamic, had spawned a rising tide of anti-Americanism in Indonesia. But the prospect of millions of dollars worth of shiny new weaponry was certainly tempting for many in Indonesia's notoriously under-funded military.

In another sign that the US was keen to get relations with Indonesia, the world's most populous Muslim country, back onto a better footing, the Bush Administration managed to invoke the war on terror in order to suppress a human rights case relating to Exxon-Mobil's involvement in Aceh. The International Labor Rights Fund (ILRF), a Washington-based organization, filed a suit against the oil giant, a huge contributor to the Republican Party, arguing it must be held accountable for its tacit involvement in Indonesia's brutal military campaign in Aceh during the 1990s. The company was accused of providing the military with buildings which were then used for torturing local people suspected of involvement in the GAM, and with excavators which it used to dig mass graves for the victims of military violence. In a *New York Times* editorial entitled 'Oily Diplomacy' on 19 August 2002, the paper accused the Bush Administration of 'promiscuously invoking the war on terrorism' after it successfully managed to get the ILRF case, which would have been an embarrassment to the Indonesian government, as well as Exxon-Mobil, dismissed on the grounds it could endanger Indonesia's cooperation in fighting terrorism.

Some involved in the Aceh mediation suspect the Exxon link may have been behind an attempt in 2001, which was thought to come from the Justice Department, to get GAM put on the US official terrorist list. They'd discovered this by accident while surfing the web. Griffiths says: 'We were deeply worried about this and we immediately got hold of our friends in the State Department and said: "This is not helpful." ' The HD Centre was assured by their friends that it wasn't going to happen.

* * * * * *

On the day that the *New York Times* was chastising the Bush Administration for exploiting its war on terror, the Indonesian government threatened to revive its own violent approach to solving GAM's insurgency. Violence in the province had continued unabated with at least 850 people being killed in the first half of 2002. The message, delivered by the Security Minister Susilo Bambang Yudhoyono, was that if their autonomy package was not accepted within three months 'the government will take stern and swift measures, including increasing the intensity of security operations, to secure the sovereignty and integrity of Indonesia'. GAM were given until 7 December 2002, the end of Ramadan, to sign up to it or face the consequences.

The publication of this deadline took Griffiths by surprise. The previous month he had met Yudhoyono in Singapore. There they had agreed to work urgently on securing an agreement and had privately decided on this time limit which was to be kept secret. It appeared that Yudhoyono, who seemed then to be personally convinced that the military operation was not succeeding, had been given a political window to revive the peace process. But, as his August announcement of a deadline revealed, he was under pressure to make it clear it would be revived only on the government's terms.

With the government publicly seizing the peace agenda, the GAM had been humiliatingly reduced to having to accept a *fait accompli*. And it seemed as if the whole process might now be derailed.

Some in the GAM were privately taking a longer-term view. They knew that, realistically, independence was not on the cards, not least because since 9/11, the US had repeatedly stressed that it fully backed the 'territorial integrity of the Republic of Indonesia'. They believed, however, that they would achieve it because they thought sooner or later Indonesia would disintegrate.

Three years after the political earthquake of East Timorese independence, in October 2000 Indonesia suffered another shock of a different nature but one which also raised questions about the stability of this complex country. On 12 October the extremist Islamic group Jemaah Islamiah planted a bomb in a nightclub in Bali which killed 202 people. The courting by the US, which Indonesia had enjoyed since 9/11, soured. American officials let it be known that Indonesia was now considered the 'weakest link' in the war on terrorism and that it had repeatedly warned Megawati that Indonesian extremists were cooperating with Al Qaeda. Yet Megawati, facing an heightened mood of anti-Americanism at home, had failed to take action. In the wake of the Bali bombing, Megawati was not just having to deal with strained foreign relations, she found herself also vulnerable on the economic front: Indonesia's tourism industry was in tatters, prospects for foreign investment looked grim and those established foreign multinational companies, including the oil producers, were jittery.

Behind the scenes, Griffiths had made it clear to Indonesian government ministers that their attempt to publicly dictate the process had only threatened to alienate the GAM and in doing so undermine the ongoing efforts to get an agreement. A week after the Bali bomb had rocked the government's credibility at home and abroad, Griffiths sensed the moment had arrived to seize back his peace process.

Griffiths, who seldom talks directly to the media, used a press conference in Banda Aceh to vent his frustration at the government for claiming the time limit they had all privately set on the Aceh negotiations, as its own. 'Yes, it was a step out of the role and I do it very rarely.'

'Dialogue should have no deadline,' he said. Then, in a move designed to take the initiative from the government and put pressure on the GAM who were by this point 'dawdling', he promptly went about and set one of his own. He gave the two sides until 9 December to sign an agreement: two days after the deadline the government had itself set.

Even though during the previous months the Centre had continued to facilitate contacts between the two sides, by issuing its own deadline it was able to 'define the process' once more. 'It was a conscious decision and it was a big risk because we had no sense of whether we would have a deal by then but we wanted to draw a line. We chose that date because it was after the deadline set by Megawati. We wanted to take control.'

Cessation of Hostilities Agreement signed

From now on things moved fast. Within two months of Griffiths' deadline, the final agreement was thrashed out. Griffiths was endlessly shuttling between the two parties. One meeting even took place at Versailles. The Cessation of Hostilities Agreement (COHA) finally signed on 9 December 2002 in Geneva was a deal to stop fighting so that actual peace talks could begin. Autonomy was the working basis of the yet-to-be struck final deal. The GAM agreed to put its weapons in 'placement sites' and the Indonesian government, in a major concession, agreed to foreign peace-keepers monitoring the implementation.

The dubious sincerity with which the parties both entered this agreement is exposed by their joint insistence that the HD Centre should be the key player in its implementation. It meant this tiny organization of academics and humanitarians would be in charge of the peace monitoring force sent from Thailand and the Philippines, as well as running the weapons collections sites. These are jobs more usually carried out by the UN department of peace-keeping, which has thousands of staff and troops and, more to the point, years of experience.

Initially Griffiths didn't want the Centre to take on the monitoring role. But there seemed no choice. The US had made it clear to the government that there would have to be international monitors for any agreement. In the final deal the Indonesian government accepted this, providing the Centre oversaw the implementation. Griffiths is aware that, despite his belief in trying to counter the imbalance of power at the negotiating table, the stronger one of the parties set the main terms and conditions of the agreement. 'The fact that they do have that right and power to choose is a problem. It's wrong, but it's simply not a level playing field.'

And so Griffiths said yes. 'Our difficulty was that we were running so fast into the December agreement, we didn't have the reflective capacity to think it through.' And with his typical frankness, Griffiths admits saying no, and risking losing the deal completely was harder still. 'It was very seductive and flattering. It made us feel as if we were really achieving something.'

While the government wanted the HD Centre to monitor the overall implementation, the GAM wanted the Centre to specifically monitor the secret locations where they would deposit their weapons. To take on these new roles, Griffiths recruited people with the right expertise. He had already brought in Rupert Smith, the respected British General who had run the UN mission in Bosnia in the mid-1990s, and from there he brought in several other former Generals, mainly from India. He even brought in a private security firm, made up of former British soldiers, to run an operations room.

Griffiths was being strongly backed not just by the US but the EU and Japan as well as he entered this untrodden area of peace-making. Everyone knew that however imperfect this agreement, and however ambivalent the parties were about its success, because of Indonesian sensitivities to foreign interference, at that point in time it was the best anyone could have hoped for. And in carving out this niche, Griffiths was defining the Centre's unique role: it is able to do what diplomats and their governments want to get done but can't be seen to do themselves.

Despite the enormous challenges, Griffiths believes that it was actually quite feasible for a small organization like the Centre to take on the implementation of the agreement. 'You just recruit the right people. It's perfectly doable. If you have the money you can do it. And actually raising the money for this wasn't difficult.' Unlike many more cautious peace mediators, he was at least prepared to risk seeing if it would work. 'We are much more inclined to throw ourselves at something than others who don't want to make a mistake. I am very sorry, in a professional way, that we didn't, in the end, have the opportunity to do it.'

The agreement falls apart

The ink was barely dry before the agreement started falling apart. The Indonesian army was not interested in losing control of the province to autonomous rule. And it took the opportunity the ceasefire provided to improve its intelligence on the GAM. The GAM, which had managed to increase its international profile and perceived legitimacy through signing the agreement, also made use of the ceasefire to regroup and reposition itself. Griffiths believes that the reasons for the agreement falling apart were multiple and complex, although Sidney Jones of the International Crisis Group (ICG) has a simple explanation. She says bluntly: 'There was no real interest on either side over the package contained in the COHA.'

The first crack to be exposed was when the GAM started putting its own particular spin on the COHA. And Griffiths, who now had an official role on the Joint Security Council, a body made up of senior members of both parties to oversee the COHA, found himself being publicly asked to arbitrate. 'Up until the peace agreement we had kept a fairly low profile. Suddenly that changed, and in January 2003 I found myself with the Governor of Aceh and government ministers telling me to "please tell the Acehnese people this deal is not about independence".' Predictably, that was exactly what the GAM was saying it was all about.

Meanwhile the government's ambivalence towards the agreement was clear in Megawati's desire to distance herself from it. 'Following one cabinet meeting while the COHA was still in place,' recalls Griffiths, 'the press asked Megawati: "How is it going in Aceh, Madam President?" She said: "I don't know, it's nothing to do with me: ask him", referring to Susilo Bambang Yudhoyono who was standing next to her.'

Lack of trust on both sides saw the implementation of the COHA crumble within three months. In December 2002 donors had pledged over $8 million to support the COHA implementation. But neither party could agree over the details of how they should demilitarize. The level of violence in the province, which had dropped dramatically immediately after the signing, began to rise. The Centre itself became a target as its staff and monitors were attacked.

After much vacillating, on 25 April 2003 the two sides agreed to meet in Geneva to try and get the implementation back on track. GAM had insisted on meeting outside of Indonesia. But when GAM asked to postpone the talks for two days, the government of Indonesia, angered that a bunch of insurgents should mess them around, refused to attend.

Tokyo, May 2003

Finally they met in Tokyo on 18 May 2003. In the run up to this meeting, hundreds of combat-ready troops had begun arriving in Aceh and Megawati had been talking about 'restoring security' in the province. Then the day before the meeting was due to take place, five GAM negotiators were arrested by the Indonesian authorities just as they were leaving Aceh en route to Tokyo. The Stockholm-based GAM, who arrived on the Friday night in Tokyo, agreed to let the talks go ahead because, Griffiths says, 'they didn't want to be a scapegoat for the talks failing'. The meeting was then delayed a further day as Griffiths, with the vital support of the US ambassador behind the scenes, spent the next 24 hours negotiating their release. But the five had only been released for the duration of the talks. 'We set up phone calls between them and GAM in Tokyo so they could participate in the talks. And afterwards they went back to jail.'

In this grim atmosphere, Griffiths, the Americans, the EU, the World Bank and the Japanese, who were hosting the talks, all tried to get the process back on track. But it was evident from the outset, says Griffiths, that they had been set up. 'The government came with demands, GAM accepted them, and then the government increased its demands. It was an absurd charade.'

By the end of the meeting, GAM recommitted itself even more boldly to what they had signed up to in the December agreement. They agreed to give up the armed struggle in favour of political struggle; participate in elections; place their weapons in accordance with the COHA provisions; cease weapons smuggling, and most significant of all, desist from advocating independence. 'By any standards it should have been enough to sustain the process,' says Griffiths who was dismayed at the Indonesian government's behaviour.

As the difficult day wore on it became increasingly clear that the Indonesians had only agreed to the meeting in order to allow it to fail. An official end to the peace process would be the pretext on which martial law could instantly be declared.

Griffiths recalls the distress of Wiryono Sastrohandoyo, Indonesia's Chief Negotiator, while giving his closing statement to the conference. 'I sensed he knew what was going to happen to the people of Aceh the next morning. And being desperately patriotic, he saw what the failure of this process would do to his country. And, of course, he must have felt that he had been forced to represent a view which he didn't like, one which could only lead to war.'

While there was widespread vexation at the behaviour of the Indonesians among the diplomats present, Griffiths was a lone voice in wanting to go public with a press statement to expose what had happened. Suddenly the difference in Griffiths' interests and that of his backers was exposed. Griffiths' sole concern was restoring the agreement and, with it, the process he had sweated so long over.

His backers, however, on whose support he depended, had more complex interests at stake. For them, peace in Aceh was simply one little square on a very large chessboard of Asia-Pacific geopolitics. It was not worth upsetting the Indonesians over this. The US, who until now had been his stalwart mediation buddy, was taken aback by the Indonesians' behaviour, but wanted to remain silent. The Japanese hosts, while privately put out at finding themselves set-up by the Indonesians to host a meeting they knew would fail, publicly presented a wall of diplomatic calm. And they were concerned to ensure that Griffiths did the same. After the meeting closed, one Japanese diplomat said to him: 'I think it's very important to take a very deep breath before doing anything.'

In retrospect, Griffiths accepts that the diplomatic instinct to say nothing was the right one. 'The question is whether it would have made any difference.' The answer was obvious. 'A strong statement would not have made the slightest bit of difference to Jakarta.'

The following day, in what the Indonesian government justified as its own 'shock and awe' approach in the fight against domestic terrorism, 40,000 troops were let loose against the GAM, following orders to 'destroy them to their roots'. Human rights groups say that in the process, the Indonesian army made no distinction between GAM members and GAM sympathizers. Two hundred schools were burned; and students, journalists and human rights campaigners randomly arrested.

One of Megawati's presidential advisors was quoted in the *New York Times* as describing the crackdown as a 'blessing of September 11'. The war on terror meant that they too could use their military might now to *legitimately* deal with insurgent groups such as GAM, in the name of counter-terrorism.

Sidney Jones of ICG says at this time 'US leverage with the Indonesia government had never been lower – nor anti-American sentiment higher.' US diplomats critical of the military crackdown against the GAM were treated with 'not just anger but with contempt by Indonesian politicians who believe they are on far stronger ground sending troops into Aceh than the US was in sending troops into Iraq'. The military crack-down, while shocking to the outside world, was popular in much of Indonesia. Domestically, the COHA had been widely criticized as a means of legitimizing the GAM, and even the HD Centre was seen in some quarters as unwelcome outside interference.

The aftermath of the collapse

In the months following the break-up of the process, Griffiths still found himself dealing with the arrest of the five GAM negotiators. He says the HD Centre went and knocked on every embassy door in Jakarta but the diplomatic community did little more than shrug. 'We were called as witness to the trial, which took place in Aceh. But the government did not allow us to attend. The only evidence that was produced in their trial – they were allegedly involved in some bombings – was that they had been members of our Joint Security Council. So they were convicted.'

In January 2004, the Aceh High Court upheld the verdict which found the five guilty of treason and terrorism, and sentenced them to between 12 and 16 years in jail. Griffiths says he felt 'terrible' about this. With efforts ongoing to revive the process Griffiths thought that perhaps they should pull out on the basis of these arrests. They asked the GAM if they should. 'They said: "Thank you very much but no, don't withdraw." Our position now is that we cannot be any part of a renewed negotiation while any of those guys are in jail. It would take a lot to persuade me not to stick to that because those guys are in jail because of us. And what about the next lot?'

'I think it's straightforward,' he adds resolutely, but then wavers as he reflects for a moment on the reality of refusing to be involved again. 'But when it comes to it, refusing to resume the negotiation process because of this, well I don't know how we will face that. At what point do you say no? Saying no is very, very difficult for a mediator.'

Since Aceh, Griffiths has been involved in many more mediations, mostly in Africa and Asia. But Aceh has left its mark on him, not just because it was his first, but because of the parties' provocative ambivalence towards their own involvement. He is only half-joking when he says he blames the experience for turning his hair grey. 'After all this, again we asked ourselves, were we complicit in a fraudulent process?'

Postscript

August 2005: a final deal is signed

Although it wasn't clear at the time, it now seems the answer to that was no. For even though the process he led for three years fell apart, it established the foundations on which the mediation would be restarted two years later. But not, this time, by Griffiths.

The change of heart from both sides came in the wake of the tsunami on 26 December 2004. In Aceh more than 100,000 people – ten times more than the total which had been killed in the 30-year conflict – died when the tidal wave engulfed much of the province's coastline. Out of the profound upheaval created by the tragedy came the possibility that some good might come of it.

In the days after the event, Griffiths, who was on holiday in Malaysia with his family, received a phone call from the Secretary General, Kofi Annan.

Since May 2003, when the military crack-down took place, the HD Centre had kept in touch with both sides. But their contacts, particularly those with the Indonesian government, had never seemed to go anywhere. While Annan wanted to know how the Centre might be able to help revive the process, in the course of the phone call he also mentioned that another peace mediator, the former Finnish President Martti Ahtisaari, had been in touch with the GAM in the previous weeks.

In the following weeks, Griffiths and his team set about trying to get things started again. Even though they managed to convince the GAM that the time was now right to negotiate, it soon became clear that neither side, not even GAM, were particularly interested in their involvement.

As it turned out, Martti Ahtisaari had been more than just in touch. He had already managed to get the two sides to agree to talk again. Griffiths shrugs: 'We thought we were taking messages,' he says, 'but after three weeks we realized the process wasn't ours anymore.' And at that moment, he was very clear: 'We are in the way, we stand down.' It was hard for the Centre's staff. 'They had got plugged in right away, of course. They had all the connections. It was hard for them to let go.'

The government and GAM needed a mediator with more clout. A month after the tsunami, Ahtisaari held his first round of talks in Helsinki. By the summer a deal was signed. Under his mediation, the GAM had been told that independence could not even be mentioned at the negotiating table. The rules of the game had changed. And, as Griffiths says, if you change the rules, you need to change the mediator. 'We were the baton passer,' he says. 'It may not sound glamorous, but it is a very useful function. It is not one that is well managed in this business, on the whole.'

On 15 August 2005, the Indonesian government signed a deal with the GAM in Helsinki. The GAM agreed to give up its aim of independence in return for self-government. Hostilities ended with the GAM committing to disarming and the government to withdrawing all but local police and military from the province. Achenese would eventually get to form local political parties and elections – monitored by the EU and the Association of Southeast Asian Nations (ASEAN) – would be held. Aceh would get to keep 70 per cent of revenue from gas and other natural resources.

Two weeks after the signing the GAM negotiators arrested on route to Tokyo in May 2003 were released as part of the deal, along with hundreds of other pro-Achenese prisoners.

Selected sources

Reports

Human Rights Watch, 'Indonesia: Human Rights, The Key to Lasting Peace in Aceh', 11 December 2002.

Edward Aspinall and Harold Crouch, *The Aceh Peace Process: Why it Failed*, The East-West Center, Washington 2003.

International Crisis Group, 'Aceh: A Fragile Peace', February 2003.

International Crisis Group, 'Resuming US–Indonesia Military Ties', ICG Briefing paper, 21 May 2002.

International Crisis Group, 'The Military Option Still Won't Work', 9 May 2003.

Kira Kay, *The 'New Humanitarianism': The Henry Dunant Center and the Aceh Peace Negotiations*, Woodrow Wilson School of Public and International Affairs, Princeton, 2004.

Pushpa Iyer and Christopher Mitchell, *The Collapse of Peace Zones in Aceh*, Institute for Conflict Analysis and Resolution, George Mason University, 2004.

Kirsten E Shultz, *The Free Aceh Movement [GAM]: Anatomy of a Separatist Organization*, East-West Center Washington, 2004.

News sources

BBC News Online: Reports and Analysis.

The Aceh Question, *PBS Online Newhour*, 12 November 1999.

'Indonesia, GAM sign Peace Agreement', *Jakarta Post*, 13 May 2000.

'Aceh rebels given peace deadline', *CNN.Com/World*, 19 August 2002.

'Dialog should have no deadline', *Jakarta Post*, 21 October 2002.

Jane Perlez, 'Indonesia says it will press attacks on separatists in Sumatra', *New York Times*, 23 May 2003.

Al Gedicks, 'Resource War in Aceh', *Z Magazine Online*, July/August 2003.

Other sources

Backgrounder on Aceh – *TAPOl*, posted on www.thinkcentre.org, August 2001.

Exxon Mobil: An American Terrorist in Aceh, JATAM, Mining Advocacy Network, August 2002.

Interview with Shadia Marhaban, coordinator of the International Network at the Aceh Referendum Information Center (SIRA), posted on www.asiasource.org.

Testimony of Sidney Jones of the International Crisis Group before Sub-committee on East Asia and the Pacific, US House of Representatives, 10 June 2003.

Transcript of Sidney Jones of ICG briefing at the USINDO Society, 11 June 2003, www.usindo.org

4 The Straight Talkers

Vidar Helgesen and Erik Solheim
Sri Lanka

Born in 1968, Vidar Helgesen studied and trained as a lawyer. Politi-
cally active from his youth, he has been long involved in Norway's
Conservative Party. As an active member of the Central Executive
Committee of Young Conservatives, his career developed to include
activities in fundraising, journalism and political advice and consulting.
Other senior appointments have included acting as Special Adviser to the
President of the International Federation of Red Cross and Red Crescent
Societies. He was appointed Norway's State Secretary and Deputy
Minister for Foreign Affairs in October 2001 and remained in those
positions October 2005.

Erik Solheim was born in 1955, and has been involved in politics from an
early age, starting with his three-year chairmanship of the Socialist Youth
League in 1977. His association with Norway's Socialist Left Party has
seen him act as Party Secretary, Chairman for ten years (1987–97) and
Member of Parliament, in which positions he has pursued ongoing
interests in foreign policy and the environment. He acted as a Special
Advisor and peace envoy to the Sri Lankan conflict of the Ministry of
Foreign Affairs from 2000. In October 2005, following a change of
government, he was appointed as Minister of International Development,
and took over Helgesen's position as Norway's head of delegation to the
Sri Lankan peace process.

Only vicars have to drink more tea in the course of their duty than
peace mediators. Well tea or coffee or Coca-Cola. On 27 July

2004, over the course of nine and three-quarter hours, Vidar Helgesen, Norway's Deputy Foreign Minister, had twelve cups. His day began at the Hilton in Colombo with one of the President's advisors and ended with a meeting with the President at her house. In between, he squeezed in the gamut of Sri Lankan society. There were religious leaders, civil society leaders, non-governmental organizations (NGOs), opposition politicians, businessmen and diplomats.

Everyone got the same message: prospects for the resumption of peace talks were grim. Even though the two-year-old ceasefire brokered by the Norwegians was still officially holding, the war it had frozen was now melting at the edges.

The evidence was plain: suicide bombers had returned to the capital. Two weeks before, five people had died in the centre of town when a woman with explosives strapped around her chest blew herself up. And despite the official ceasefire, killings were taking place again. Just that week, eight renegade Tamil Tiger rebels had been executed in a leafy Colombo suburb. Despite the alarming events, few of the Sri Lankans Helgesen debriefed seem too disturbed by developments. After telling a group of businessmen that the country's frozen conflict was melting at the edges he wryly wondered what affect this might have on the stock market. It had none.

Much to Helgesen's frustration, it seemed the ceasefire, the Norwegian's persisting prize in the stumbling process, was being treated by many in the relatively prosperous city of Colombo as a proxy peace. And a proxy peace breeds lethargy. The kind of lethargy which leaves parties in no hurry to return to the negotiating table.

Norway first found out it had got the job as Sri Lanka's official peace facilitator when watching TV. It was the end of December 1999, and President Chandrika Kumaratunga was giving an interview to the BBC, her first since losing an eye in an assassination attempt by the Tamil Tigers two weeks earlier. She used the occasion not to condemn her potential murderers, but to announce that secret peace talks were already under way.

'It was a complete surprise to us,' recalls Erik Solheim, then the Norwegian government's special envoy and first main facilitator of the process. The Norwegians had been involved in secret negotiations about negotiations for months.

The process started when the Liberation Tigers of Tamil Eelam (LTTE) rebels, more commonly known as the Tamil Tigers, had got in touch with the Norwegians to ask if they could evacuate their senior advisor, and later Chief Negotiator, Anton Bala-singham, to a third county on medical grounds. The LTTE hinted that if this were done, it might lead onto a peace process.

So Norway set about getting permission from the Sri Lankan government to get Balasingham out. This led to a series of secret meetings between the then Norwegian Ambassador in Colombo, Jon Westborg, and Kumaratunga and the Foreign Minister, Lakshman Kadirgamar, who was assasinated in the summer of 2005. 'No one knew about these talks, not even the Prime Minister,' says Solheim. In the end Balasingham, who was suf-fering from acute diabetes, was brought out by the LTTE on one of their ships in the late summer of 1999. Since then he has lived in London.

But these contacts were enough to establish the Norwegians as potential facilitators to end a conflict which had been going on since 1983. Tensions between the Sinhala majority and Tamil minority population had been simmering since Sri Lanka was granted independence in 1948 in a wave of Sinhalese nationalism. Over the subsequent decades tensions increased as repeated governments imposed policies marginalizing the Tamil minority, which today makes up just 13 per cent of the population. In the mid-1950s, Sinhala was declared the only official language and later Buddhism was recognized as the country's main religion. In 1976, amid increasing ethnic tension, the LTTE was formed and started demanding a separate Tamil state.

The current conflict dates back to the deaths of 13 Sri Lankan army soldiers in an LTTE ambush in 1983. It sparked a wave of brutal rioting across the south of the country in which hundreds of Tamils were killed and thousands more fled the country. Many of those who failed to flee the country fled north to the relative safety of the Tamil majority areas. The LTTE managed to take control of the north part of the island, effectively sealing it off from the rest of the country.

In the late 1980s, India, the regional power, attempted its own peace process. It ended disastrously with its peace-keeping force having to leave after becoming embroiled in fighting with the Tamil Tigers. Norway was careful to get India's approval before trying her own hand at peace, a decade later.

The Norwegian's new role as peace-makers in Sri Lanka got off to a depressing start. During that first year, 2000, the country saw some of the heaviest fighting of the war. In April the LTTE successfully launched an offensive to capture the strategically vital Elephant's Pass, which links the mainland to the Jaffna peninsula. In September, in one of the biggest military operations of the war, the Sri Lankan army won it back. Thousands were killed on both sides.

Solheim questions whether you could 'even talk of a peace process at that time'. Despite the all-out war, the Norwegians remained working, doing what they could to ameliorate the viciousness of the fighting, pushing for access for humanitarian aid in rebel areas and the release of prisoners of war. Solheim says: 'We did what we could to avoid misunderstandings between the parties. We kept in close contact with both sides, passing messages between them. But there were no physical meetings whatsoever between the two sides at that time.

'In this first phase, we saw our role as that of the listener. We listened to both sides, tried to understand their concerns, and spoke much less than we listened.'

From this time on in the process, Norway staked out its ground on the sidelines of the conflict. It made it clear that it would only get more deeply involved when asked. 'Remember, Norway has no way of imposing peace in Sri Lanka, we have no marines to send, we are not a military power, we do not even have any meaningful way of putting diplomatic pressure on them. We can only assist them if they so wish.'

Both the government and Tigers trot out the same reasons for choosing this small Nordic country to resolve their differences. Firstly, they have no regional or historical interest in the country. Secondly, it was already experienced at peace mediation, the Middle East being the most commonly cited example. Thirdly, it had established ties with Sri Lanka through its development projects, and because of this was seen to understand the country to some extent.

There are two further factors which make Norway uniquely useful in the peace industry. It has money, which it is prepared to invest – and risk – in all types of peace initiatives, not only ones in which it is directly involved. And, just as importantly, when it does this, it takes a long-term view. This is because Norway enjoys a culture of consensual politics which itself is so lacking in conflict that the management of a lengthy peace process is simply not affected by a change in government. Such is the political calm of the place, that an outsider might wonder what is.

For the consensual nature of Norwegian politics is extra-ordinary. And it is as cosy as it is consensual. Until the autumn of 2005, the Prime Minister was Kjell Magne Bondevik. He is a Christian Democrat who is also a Lutheran minister, and he plays football with Erik Solheim (of the Socialist Left Party) every Thursday morning at 7am. He also conducted Erik's wedding to his second wife, who belongs to the Conservative Party. Vidar Helgesen is also a member of the Conservative Party and works, of course, shoulder to shoulder with Erik. Erik became involved in the Sri Lanka process because he happened to be staying at the Sri Lankan home of his friend Arne Fjortoft when early contacts about possible Norwegian involvement took place. As well as being an old friend, Arne was also an old political adversary, having been Chairman of Norway's Liberal Party, and as such previously battled Erik (who was Chairman of his party) for Norway's environmental vote.

In a country of four and a half million people, it's not surprising to find a closely-knit political elite. But Norwegians are quick to claim that as a new country (it is just 100 years old) it does not – unlike its former colonizer Sweden – have an upper class or, indeed, an elite. But these people are an elite of sorts, pulled together, if not by an excluding wealth, than by a common motivation. The phrase they all often use, when asked why they do this kind of work, is 'to be of use'.

Peace mediation has successfully given Norway, normally a minor player on the world stage, a much enhanced international profile. They claim their place with a shameless morality – Helgesen once told a human rights seminar: 'In the global village, the security and prosperity of each human being is a responsibility for all.' And with touching modesty he went on to tell them: 'As a very small country, we cannot be the policeman of that global village. We cannot be the fire brigade. But we can be a kind of social worker.'

Down a narrow corridor at the Norwegian Foreign Ministry in Oslo, Erik Solheim works full time maintaining the Norwegian's peace facilitation in Sri Lanka. His office overflows with piles of books and papers; every minute the phone rings and his computer is constantly beeping with emails dropping into his inbox. It seems even maintaining a stalled peace process – it is more than a year since any talks actually took place – is a hectic business.

In this endearing chaos, Solheim has mislaid the teabags. With an apologetic grin he eventually finds them caught up in a pile of documents and starts boiling water in a travel kettle under his desk. It is easy to see why Solheim has a reputation for being popular with the Tamil Tigers, a group known for shunning contact with the outside world. He has a shiny warmth and informality not common among diplomats. In that early stage of the process, Solheim impressed the Tigers and some members of the government with his deep understanding of their history and their concerns. He spent so much time with them that by his own admission what began as formal relationships evolved into friendships. Solheim argues this was good for the process. 'The benefits of having friendships clearly outweighs the disadvantages. I believe the more you know them the more you come to understand the conflict, the more able you will be able to play a role. And a personal relationship may help in finding a way round difficult issues at the negotiating table.'

Not everyone agreed. He came under criticism from senior members of the Sri Lankan government, including Kumaratunga herself, who considered him too close to the Tigers. But it emerged it wasn't just that. As a Special Envoy to the process, a position which still gives him the rank of a civil servant, Solheim wasn't important enough for her.

The facilitation process had been rumbling on for 18 months without significant progress. The sticking point was the lifting of the ban on the LTTE. The LTTE demanded it be a precondition of talks. Kumaratunga's government said it could happen only once talks were under way. In June 2001, according to a report in the Indian magazine *Frontline*, the government issued an 'urgent invitation' to Norway's then Foreign Minister, Thorbjorn Jagland. Accompanied by Solheim, he was able to spare just a few hours for this unscheduled trip, during which time he had dinner with the President and left. In what was a clear snub, Solheim was not invited to that dinner.

With her Foreign Minister, Lakshman Kadirgamar at her side, Kumaratunga told Jagland that she was not happy with Solheim's success rate so far and felt he had exhausted his usefulness in the process. No one questioned Solheim's integrity but it was felt that he had become rather partial to the LTTE. But far from wanting to push the Norwegians out, she wanted to upgrade their involvement, saying she felt that a more senior level of engagement could get things kick-started. As exaggerated media reports of these events spread, unhelpfully for Solheim, the LTTE waded in to his defence.

The LTTE issued a statement, in which it firstly accused Norway of breaching protocol by failing to consult them on the change in facilitation roles. It then went on to talk of Solheim's 'impeccable neutrality', accusing the government of using the 'ploy' of upgrading Norway's role in order to 'downgrade and marginalize' Solheim's. Anton Balasingham added weight to this by telling a Sri Lankan paper that the government had meted out 'shabby, unfair and insulting' treatment to the envoy. As *Frontline* argued, 'Whatever the merits of the LTTE statement, it helped re-enforce suspicion among the Sinhala ultra-nationalists that Solheim was in cahoots with the Tigers.'

In the weeks that followed, the Prime Minister suggested Solheim should withdraw from the mediation, and some voices in parliament echoed this, with Buddhist nationalists demanding he be declared *persona non grata*.

But the Norwegians weathered the storm, keeping Solheim on board, and at the end of it all they had emerged with an enhanced role to play.

One of the many complaints the government had levelled against Solheim was over the time he had spent bonding with the leader of the opposition party, Ranil Wickremesinghe. Any mediator who is in a process for the long haul needs to do this, however uncomfortable it makes the current government. In the end it proved fruitful groundwork – in December 2001 – his party narrowly won the general election and Wickremesinghe became Prime Minister. In contrast to his predecessor, he was very serious about talking peace.

Within a month of his taking office, unilateral ceasefires, first by the LTTE, then by the government, had been called. By the end of February 2002 this informal ceasefire had been formalized into an agreement which included a military ceasefire, a number of confidence-building measures, and the setting up of a Sri Lankan

Monitoring Mission made up of a mix of Nordic countries and headed by the Norwegians. The confidence-building measures included the opening up of the road from Colombo to the north, which after years of isolation brought on by fighting was deeply impoverished and widely destroyed.

The general election may have brought in a new government, but it kept the country with its old President. And along with the peace process began a deeply uneasy cohabitation between arch political rivals Kumaratunga and Wickremasinghe which would prove as much a threat to the peace process as the resumption of war.

Kumaratunga was furious that she had been excluded by her Prime Minister from the signing of the ceasefire agreement. The Norwegians had taken a calculated risk in accepting this. In a formal sense they had no alternative, since the head of government also headed the peace process for the government side. In a practical sense, trying to let Kumaratunga share some of the credit for Wickremasinghe's peace coup would have been a non-starter. The two were sworn enemies. But in facilitating negotiations that excluded her, the Norwegians would have to weather the consequences. Everyone knew Kumaratunga would struggle to support a peace process which was not hers.

Helgesen says they did what they could not to isolate her: 'We had meetings with the President but the one in charge was the Prime Minister. So what we could tell the President was limited, which is an awkward situation because she is Head of State. But that is how we did it, much to the displeasure of some in her party, and some in the press.'

Over the following 18 months they managed successfully to keep Kumaratunga and her complicated political baggage out of the process, and during this time things moved forward.

Before either side would sit down at the negotiating table, two things had to happen. The LTTE had to be willing to negotiate on the basis of a compromise solution short of its long-held goal of independence. And the government had to lift the ban on the LTTE. Getting the LTTE to agree to no longer insist on their claim for independence in the negotiations was an issue the Norwegians had raised from the start. Solheim says: 'If the LTTE could not be satisfied with something less than a state there was no need to start talks because a separate state can only be established by military means.' The Norwegians managed it. But it was a coup for which Solheim does not readily take credit. 'It was not us getting them to give up anything. They recognized that the aim of the peace process would be a compromise.'

Once the ceasefire was signed, the LTTE took a step towards the prospect of political acceptability in the most flamboyant way it could. For the first time in 15 years, the head of the LTTE, Velupillai Prabhakaran, made a public appearance at a press conference. For the Tigers, Prabhakaran is an enigmatic leader. For many others, he is one of the world's most wanted terrorists.

In his own country, he has a 200-year prison sentence hanging over him for bombing of the Central Bank in Colombo in 1996. There is an extradition order on him from India, where he is wanted for the murder of former President Rajiv Ghandi. He is wanted for the murder of Sri Lankan President Premadasa in 1993, and the attempted murder of the current President, Chandrika Kumaratunga, in 1999. Prabhakaran is seen as the mastermind behind the Tigers' repeated suicide bombings in the capital in which many hundreds of civilians have died, a poisonous art which the Tigers are credited as having perfected. Prabhakaran famously wears a cyanide capsule around his neck, to be taken in the event of capture. All his cadres are expected to do the same.

The organization of the LTTE is known to be bitterly ruthless. It is monolithic, some say Stalinist, in the way it seeks to maintain its position as 'sole representative' of the Tamil people by systematically killing off the opposition.

After waiting ten hours at a secret location in the jungle for him to appear, Prabhakaran eventually told the bunch of sweaty journalists that the LTTE were 'sincerely and seriously committed to peace'. But he added they would only take part in peace talks once they had been de-proscribed. 'That is the problem,' he said.

It was also the problem of the Wickremesinghe government. Wickremesinghe was quick to publicly respond positively to Prabhakaran's olive branch, saying his statement showed the LTTE 'are willing to work within the territorial integrity of the country'. But politically his position was getting more complex. President Kumaratunga had already expressed 'concerns' about the ceasefire, ominously claiming that she could use her presidential powers to annul it with just 'one letter to the Army Commander'. Kumaratunga then went one step further: she declared she would prevent a ban on the LTTE from being lifted. This would have been a popular move among many of Colombo's political factions, not least the influential National Conference of Buddhist Monks.

Ignoring the President, the government lifted the ban on the LTTE on 4 September and the LTTE followed suit by agreeing to enter negotiations on a compromise solution which would fall short of full independence. The way for talks to start was now clear.

The first round of talks was held in Sattahip, Thailand in September 2002. But before the Norwegians could get the parties to talk peace they had to get them to agree on the format for the opening ceremony – at which the international media as well as a complete diplomatic line up of ambassadors would be present.

The first issue they had to address was whether or not there would be flags on the table. There was a bit of a history over what seems a trivial issue: it had been a sticking point during a round of peace negotiations in the mid-1990s. Solheim says it matters to the parties because at a time like this they are being watched very closely: 'If the LTTE put a flag on the table, people might then say the government's side has accepted that flag and so have accepted their claim of a separatist state. Or the government may insist that if they have a flag, we should have a bigger flag because we are a government and they are a rebel movement.'

The solution was simple: no flags. 'Of course the negotiators understand the stupidity of this but the press could make it a tremendous issue.' And as the Norwegians were to learn over the coming months, no one would be keener to see the peace process fail than Sri Lanka's unruly nationalist press.

But the trouble of the opening ceremony protocol wasn't over yet. The order of seating and speeches hadn't been addressed. The Norwegians suggested the government spoke first because 'the government is the government and it's first in order of rank', but to compensate the LTTE could sit in the middle. 'And this created a problem because the Thais said this is not acceptable. This is Thailand and in Thailand the government is always of higher rank and so must sit in the middle.' The Norwegians put their foot down over this and as facilitators took responsibility for sorting out the seating arrangements themselves.

Over the following months the Norwegians arranged six sessions of talks. GL Peiris, the government's Chief Negotiator, says the intensity of the process – the parties were meeting nearly every month – helped to develop a rapport between them. 'The growth of confidence is an incremental process. When we met in September 2002 in Thailand you could see there was reserve. Not hostility but there was no rapport, trust or confidence. But then it developed over time.'

At the Sattahip base, the Thai navy from the Admiral downwards quit their homes for three days to allow the parties to move in. The head of delegations were each given a Commander's bungalow, while the more junior negotiators stayed in the base's small hotel. One of these junior negotiators says: 'Of course we were all rather uncomfortable with each other during that first round.' Rooms were on separate floors and during meals in the hotel's restaurant the two sides would awkwardly acknowledge one another with stiff hand shakes and forced small talk.

But six months later, at the Intercontinental Hotel in Berlin, the atmosphere had changed. 'We were on a buddy level by that time,' says the junior negotiator. No one cared about the protocol any longer, rooms were no longer on separate floors, they had their meals together, and went out for dinner at night. And with each round the two negotiating teams got more and more pally. 'By the sixth round we were having Jacuzzis together!'

The Norwegians avoid using the word mediation where they can. They prefer the word facilitation. This means booking the hotels, arranging flights, sorting out dates, passing messages, chairing meetings. They will do all they can to enable the two sides to talk peace – if they want to.

So, in Sri Lanka they kept up the pace of the process by arranging intense rounds of negotiation, one after another. But they did not attempt to define which direction talks would go. Helgesen says they don't see that as their role. 'We are not driving the agenda. We don't have a blueprint which we feel would be the best solution.' So what was Norway's role?

Milinda Moragoda, one of the senior government negotiators, says it was an advantage that the Norwegians themselves were under no pressure to deliver something by a certain date. 'It meant that they could allow the parties to move at their own pace. But when they felt that, in Helgesen's words, things were getting "lethargic" they would push harder. That sense of timing is the skill: to know when to do it without being seen to be overbearing.'

Instead, the Norwegians acted more as advisors to the process they ran, helping the parties to shape an agreement which would be acceptable to the international community. Helgesen says: 'We see it as our role to explain to the parties, not least the LTTE, which is not used to the workings of the international system, what they can and can't expect. We have to explain to them the rules of the game and by doing that in a very frank manner we can contribute in a productive way to achieving the same goals.'

The senior negotiators in both parties who have got to know Helgesen and Solheim well over the years appreciated their style. Peiris describes them as handling the talks with 'great finesse and subtlety'. But it is the Tigers who are particularly enthusiastic about them. Puleedevan, the LTTE's chief spokesman, proudly echoes a phrase used derisively by the Colombo press when he says: 'We call them the white Tigers.' Paper might be a better description but, nonetheless, the LTTE's passion for the Norwegians is a mixed blessing for them. As one of the facilitating team said with a sigh: 'It doesn't always help promote the image that we are, in fact, neutral.'

The parties credit the Norwegians with stepping in and keeping the negotiations going during the times it looked certain that they would fall apart. Tamilselvan, the head of the LTTE political wing, says: 'During those crisis periods, the way in which the Norwegians handled the situation helped ensure that the ceasefire agreement remained intact and the talks continued.'

One such instance was at the Berlin round of talks in February 2003. As the parties gathered at the Norwegian Embassy where the talks were due to be held, it was not sure that they would, in fact, take place. Just hours before, three Tamil Tigers had blown themselves up when their trawler, carrying an anti-aircraft gun, was cornered by a Sri Lankan naval ship. 'Tempers were running high, the LTTE were very angry,' remembers GL Peiris. 'It looked as if that round of talks would be a total failure, and indeed that the process might even collapse.'

The first thing the Norwegians did was to arrange talks between the two Chief Negotiators Anton Balasingham and Peiris in order to 'lower the temperature'. Peiris says: 'The advantage of it was that things that would have otherwise been said on the conference floor did not have to be said there because they had been taken up and sorted out beforehand. 'It meant the mood was much better.'

Secondly, they addressed the issue of a hungry media, poised to run stories of a collapsing peace process. As one of the government negotiators says: 'The press were waiting to get something juicy and antagonistic.' The Norwegians responded by helping the parties draft a joint statement which expressed the mutual 'concern' of the parties over the incident which had led to the 'tragic' loss of three lives. The bluff of the press was called. 'The statement saved the peace process.'

At times like this, the parties credit Helgesen with a fine capacity to 'soothe ruffled feathers'. Milinda Moragoda says he was a skilled chairman and a modest one: 'He was able to help give the discussion focus without himself becoming one of the egos in the process.'

Some of the negotiators, such as Moragoda, say that through the process they became friends with the Norwegians. 'We have formed good friendships, close friendships, and I think it was based on trust.' Helgesen agrees that both institutional and personal trust are vital, but he would not go as far as saying these were friendships. 'One shouldn't establish friendship-like relations because you might become too close. And if you were to establish friendships you would need to do it in a politically balanced way,' he says, adding 'and then it would be basically flawed as far as friendship goes.'

Drawing formal lines between himself and the parties is a natural extension for Helgesen from being a Minister of State. The rank this gives him has been tremendously important for both parties. For the Tigers, it has been a proxy recognition because Helgesen represents a government. For the Sri Lankan government negotiators, three of whom were themselves ministers, it was a question of their own status and respect. 'For our side, the fact he was a minister helped immensely. He had the status. They were talking to a counterpart,' said one of the government team.

Despite his desire to keep his involvement in the talks formal, he never managed to keep his personal life completely separate from the process. Both parties gave him wedding presents when he got married in June 2004. And when his mother died 18 months earlier, the LTTE sent a wreath to the funeral. 'It is one of the strange paradoxes of my current life that my mother, who was not politically active, had flowers at her funeral from what many consider to be an arch terrorist organization,' says Helgesen with a gentle smile.

Vidar Helgesen did not grow up as part of Norway's political elite to which he now belongs. His father was a salesman and his mother worked in a Salvation Army project for alcoholics. At first Helgesen seems overly formal and rather rigid – like his thick silk tie. Perhaps because, having become a government minister at the age of 32, what he lacked in years was somehow made up in a display of gravitas. But it doesn't take long for his humour to come spilling out. Every few sentences his quiet voice stumbles into a laugh. Not a hearty, loud laugh, but something soft and dry. It's evident that underneath his solemn front he actually loves what he does. Asked if he would like a second term in office, he simply replies he couldn't imagine having a better job.

During the six rounds of talks which took place between September 2002 and March 2003 the parties discussed power sharing, a federal constitution, development finance, child soldiers and, in the last round in Hakone, Japan, the possibility of a joint document on human rights.

But the process suddenly stalled in April 2003 when the LTTE pulled out. The official reason was because it had not been invited to a meeting in Washington – where it is a banned organization – to plan for a big donor conference which was to be held in Tokyo in June that year.

The lull in the peace process had left the news hungry press in Colombo desperate for a bite. In May 2003 the Prime Minister of Norway, Kjell Magne Bondevik, innocently threw them a titbit on which both Sri Lankan politicians and the press feasted. He had been asked by a journalist if Sri Lanka should be more flexible in dealing with the LTTE. All he had replied was: 'I hope so, yes.'

This caused uproar in Colombo. A Kumaratunga loyalist, and spokesman for the People's Alliance, Sarath Amunugama, was one of many to take offence. 'He is not the imperial master of Sri Lanka,' he said. One of the President's close aides, Mangala Samaraweera, waded in by publicly labelling the Norwegians 'salmon-eating busybodies'. It is a phrase that has stuck. When asked about this, Helgesen dryly remarked: 'I had no idea that Norwegian salmon had that level of brand recognition in Sri Lanka.'

It's easy to get the feeling in Sri Lanka's widely xenophobic press that all foreigners are essentially salmon-eating busybodies. With ultimate diplomacy, Helgesen politely describes the Sri Lankan media as 'creative'. 'Creative is a polite way of putting it,' says one of the Colombo-based foreign journalists, who believes the press directly damaged the peace process. 'In fact, in cahoots with the army and Kumaratunga's opposition, some of the Sri Lankan press played a very destructive role in undermining the peace process and the Wickremesinghe government.' Misquoting and quoting out of context is a speciality; and failing that, diplomats complain, journalists will simply make a story up from scratch. Meanwhile, BBC-style *balanced* news reporting, in which both sides of the story are told, is constantly condemned and even derided in the press as pro-LTTE.

The media's feral attitude has extended to anyone who has tried to come in as support for the Norwegians. In 2003 both the then EU Commissioner Chris Patten and the former Finnish President Martti Ahtisaari got their fingers burnt. In August, the *Island* ran a headline screaming: 'Keep Patten out of the country' and accused him of 'bloody European gumption and insolence of the highest order' for meeting Prabhakaran on what happened, by chance, to be his birthday. In the same month, the *Daily Mirror* tried to make diplomatic mischief by suggesting Ahtisaari had told Kumaratunga that the Norwegians 'should not overstay' in their efforts at peace.

The realities of working under this level of criticism, which diplomats are certainly not trained for, has created a survivalist attitude in the facilitating team. As one of them put it, 'If you want to get involved in this process you should expect not to get you fingers burnt, you should expect to get them electrocuted.'

The hostility of the press to the peace process hasn't just affected the Norwegians; it seems to have affected how readers vote. Since the Norwegian's started facilitating the peace process, the support for the two major parties, which in principle both support it, has diminished in favour of minority parties, many of which do not.

In July 2004, after four days of fruitlessly telling people that Sri Lanka faced 'a frozen war melting at the edges', a frustrated Helgesen met the press. One EU diplomat said he'd never heard him so forceful when he told the journalists gathered in the garden of a trendy café: 'I am disturbed about the level of violence but I am equally disturbed about the incredible complacency.' The next morning's headlines declared: 'Norway admits failure on reviving peace process'.

Although she was responsible for starting the peace process and bringing in the Norwegians, Kumaratunga had been angered by her exclusion from the peace process from the day the ceasefire was signed by her political rival Wickremesinghe until the day she dismissed his government.

This anger appeared directed at the Norwegians as well. Within a month of the ceasefire agreement she had issued a statement accusing the Norwegians of going beyond their mandate. She told Prime Minster Wickremesinghe in a letter that in the ceasefire agreement the Norwegians had gone 'far beyond the role of facilitator'. So much so, she claimed, that their status was now 'incompatible with the sovereign status of Sri Lanka'.

By October 2003 Kumaratunga was calling for the Norwegian General who headed the island's monitoring mission to be sacked. In a letter to the Norwegian Prime Minister, she accused the Sri Lankan Monitoring Mission (SLMM) of leaking information to the Tigers about a naval operation to intercept an LTTE ship, which was suspected of carrying arms.

For Kumaratunga the last straw came in early November. On 1 November, the Tigers, who had officially withdrawn from the process six months earlier, came back on the scene when they put forward their own proposal for self-government, known as the Interim Self-Governing Authority.

Kumaratunga, seething after months of exclusion from the process she believed by rights to be hers, made her move to get it back. Three days later, on 4 November, while Wickremesinghe was in Washington on an official visit, she used her presidential powers to take over the three key government ministries: defence, interior and information. Each one was centrally involved in the peace process. She suspended parliament for 15 days and put troops on alert.

The official reason for the removal was 'to prevent further deterioration of the security situation'. She said Wickremesinghe was threatening Sri Lanka's integrity by making too many concessions to the LTTE. Frances Harrison of the BBC described it as a 'constitutional coup against the government'. She added: 'It's hard to see how Mr Wickremesinghe can actually now govern this country.'

Even though her own party had dismissed the LTTE's proposal as a stepping-stone to partition, Kumaratunga, recovering her composure, said later that day that 'I remain willing to discuss with the LTTE a just and balanced solution of the national problem, within the parameters of the unity, territorial integrity and sovereignty of Sri Lanka.'

Kumaratunga's behaviour demonstrated the extent to which the issue of peace with the north is a cheap political football which Colombo's political parties kick around and use to score points off one another. But the issue of who would get to sign the deal with the LTTE was a particularly sensitive one for Kumaratunga, for she had long ridden on a political peace ticket. In 1994 she came to power claiming she would bring peace to the country. And in 2000 she was the one who had invited the Norwegians to be involved.

Chandrika Kumaratunga is not your average President. Her parents were both Prime Ministers – in fact her mother was the world's first woman ever to hold the post. At one point when she was President, she even reappointed her mother as Prime Minister. She is used to being in control. One diplomat said her motives were obvious: 'She was jealous. It looked like her arch rival was going to get the credit for peace. And so she put a stop to it.'

Kumaratunga's supporters claim the process as led by Wickremesinghe was leading to secession, or at least to more concessions to the LTTE than the southern polity could ever accept, and this itself might have been a recipe for war.

In any case, the confusion in the country was compounded the following day by the President firstly declaring a state of emergency, and then denying ever having done so. Nonetheless, the capital saw a return to the pre-ceasefire days with checkpoints being re-established, and troops being put onto the streets and deployed around key government buildings.

Wickremesinghe returned to Colombo declaring 'the whole peace process is at risk'. Wickremesinghe said he needed the Defence portfolio for it to continue. In an interview with the *Financial Times*, the President said she had had no choice but to take over defence. She claimed that since the ceasefire, the government had turned a blind eye while the LTTE brought in shipments of arms and surrounded a main naval base on the east coast. 'They,' she said, referring to the government, 'allowed the LTTE to do things that no sovereign state would ever dream of permitting.'

In a joint visit, on 10 November, Vidar Helgesen and Erik Solheim waded into this mess. Four days later, in an unprecedented display of public frustration, the Norwegians let it be known that in these circumstances they could no longer do their job and would 'go home and wait' until the political dust clouds in Colombo had settled. Helgesen said at the time that the talks could have resumed 'tomorrow' if there had been 'clarity' on who was in charge of the peace process. 'Until such clarity is re-established there is no space for further efforts by the Norwegian

14 NOV

government to assist the parties,' he said, and with that boarded a plane back to Oslo, leaving a stunned Colombo in his wake.

Looking back on it now he says: 'It was the only thing to do. We made it clear to the Prime Minister and the President that until we know what number to call in Colombo, there was nothing more we can do.' While in Colombo, they had come under pressure to mediate between the Prime Minister and the President. They refused, saying it was well beyond their mandate. If they had done that, he says: 'In all likelihood we would be left with the blame for the ongoing crisis.'

Helgesen believes that leaving at that stage actually increased respect for Norway's involvement and dampened down the habit, common among both the media and politicians, of 'Norway bashing'. 'We demonstrated that Norway is not in this for Norway's sake. We are not hanging in there just because it gives us a good name internationally – we are doing this to be of use. It was helpful because there had been a tendency to take Norway for granted.'

The public image of the Norwegian's peace mediation is unusual in that it is not a one-man band but a two-man show. Some of the negotiators, at least, believe that Helgesen and Solheim's differing personalities have been a positive thing. 'Vidar is able to focus on issues and keeps the structure going. Erik performs a complementary role in being able to handle the networks well and being confident with the people concerned. The two passing the ball to one another has worked well,' says Moragoda.

But Helgesen is keen to stress the importance of the team in the Norwegian's approach to peace mediation. And at the end of a ten-hour day of back-to-back meetings, as Helgesen and his crew relax over a bottle of wine at the Ambassador's residence, the lack of formality and hierarchy, which is so commonly dominant in other diplomatic circles, is striking.

The parties agree its been a team effort. 'You cannot under-estimate the role of each of them,' Moragoda adds. These included the Ambassador in Sri Lanka, Jon Westborg, who later left to become Ambassador in Delhi. He was known for a subtle diplomatic approach, says Solheim, stressing the importance of their mix of skills. 'No one individual can do it.' Helgesen says the varying relations different members have with each side 'enables you to play out different cards and I think that is quite essential'.

But far from having a reputation for playing a stealthy hand, the Norwegians are collectively talked about as being utterly straight. 'Helgesen is a man of immense integrity,' says one of the negotiators. 'He was undoubtedly in my mind, vital to saving the peace process.'

Honesty is an important theme for the Norwegians. Solheim says when conveying messages between the parties they are totally transparent. 'If we get a negative message we convey it even if it is absolutely unpleasant. We may take out the invectives but the core of the matter we must convey otherwise they will not trust us.' This straight-talking is, by their own admission, a natural Norwegian trait. As Solheim says: 'Norwegians tend to be blunt and honest rather than polite and indirect. The benefit of this is that we tend to speak the truth and say what we think and, in the long run, people tend to trust us. We never lie to the parties or do anything behind their backs because if we did that we would be finished.'

After months and months of a stalled process some say that it is precisely because they have done nothing behind anyone's backs that some, particularly in the south, now consider their peace effort to be 'finished'. It's not that they have lost trust in the Norwegians, it's that they have lost faith that in the fickle world of Sri Lankan politics their self-confessed straight-talking, strait-laced approach works.

Norway's unfrilly style of diplomacy, driven by a deep belief in egalitarianism, sits with an awkward charm in a country where even the rebels have their guests served tea by waiters in white gloves. Their straight-talking approach stands out starkly in Sri Lanka's multi-layered, multicultural society, which is held together by a sophisticated tradition of *politesse*, antiquated etiquette and innuendo.

While their straightness may be crucial for maintaining the parties' trust in them, it has been an irritant in some quarters. For some on the government side, the Norwegians' hands-off approach – their reluctance to do more than continue carrying messages between the two sides as a means of kick-starting the stalled process – has been deeply frustrating. 'They are so workmanlike in their approach; despite months of nothing moving their tactics have not changed. They just seem to lack the necessary oomph to get the things going again,' said one diplomatic source.

And what they might call their bluntness or transparency is for others their naïvety. One of the government side says: 'They think there is something pure about being facilitators. They really believe that they are neutral and separate from the process. But they are part of it.'

Much too much so, according to some in Colombo. It is inevitable that any peace mediator will at some point be accused of bias. And, knowing the LTTE are an outlawed terrorist organization in many parts of the world, having the Norwegians pay them visits on a regular basis has been hard to stomach for many Sri Lankans from the south. The Norwegians certainly talk with compassion for the plight of a people who have for a generation been impoverished and degraded by war. Moreover, Solheim especially, knowing the LTTE so well, talks with a tenderness for a people who are themselves trapped in a merciless regime.

Asked what was the most difficult aspect of this job, Solheim responds: 'The completely different worlds these people are living in. Most of the LTTE leaders are military people. They have spent their entire adult life fighting to achieve their vision in the jungles of northern Sri Lanka. They speak Tamil. They do not speak

Sinhalese. They do not understand English. And so their outlook is, of course, confined to a Tamil perspective.'

This comparison with the government side is stark. 'Many Sinhalese leaders are travelling around the world. They are very global in their outlook. They come from an elite.'

And then Solheim makes a point which explains why Sri Lankan politicians are so ready to use the process not for peace, but to score political points off one another. 'They are very far from the war: hardly anyone from the middle class, let alone the upper class, are in the army.' What he means is that the lives of their sons are not at risk. 'So there is a big big gap. To create some kind of trust, some kind of bridge between them is extremely difficult.'

LTTE territory is certainly a world away from Colombo with its swish hotels and sushi bars. During the eight-hour drive north, the wealth visibly drains from the landscape. By the time you cross the checkpoint into LTTE-controlled country there are no private cars, no solid houses, no fast roads. Just shacks and bicycles, trucks and the occasional aid worker's Toyota Land Cruiser bumping over potholed roads.

In July 2004, Helgesen took a helicopter to Kilinochi to discuss with the Tigers how things might be put back on track. But the events of the previous day – police had found the bodies of eight men from the breakaway faction led by Karuna, a former senior LTTE commander – dominated the initial conversation. Having split from the LTTE in March 2004, Karuna led the thousands of troops who remained loyal to him in a hopeless battle against the LTTE. Having been roundly defeated, his troops scattered, he was thought to have gone underground in Colombo.

Helgesen arrived on the dusty sports ground the Tigers use as a helicopter pad to be told his meeting was delayed. So to help time pass, the Norwegians were offered elevenses at the LTTE guest house. Seated around a table laden with plates of sliced mango, papaya, pineapple, cakes and biscuits, Seevarathnam Puleedevan, the Tiger's amiable head of the peace secretariat, played host at this slightly awkward tea party. Puleedevan is a man who smiles as much as he breathes. On this occasion, he strived to use his jovial manner to keep the atmosphere, if not the conversation, light.

The events of the previous day were the obvious subject for the small talk. Being up to speed with the goings-on, the Norwegian Ambassador to Sri Lanka, Hans Brattskar, fired off the questions. While white-gloved waiters hovered, serving tea and instant coffee, Puleedevan sailed through questions on the reason for the assassinations, the apparent lack of resistance to the executions, and the security implications of the killings, in between mouthfuls of mango, without the smile ever falling from his face.

With a little huff of frustration, one of the Norwegian team admitted afterwards they had been told them nothing that they had not already read that morning in the papers.

The LTTE were the prime suspects in the killing of these disloyal Tigers. Famed for a culture of ruthlessness, the LTTE had continued to bump off alternative Tamil opposition politicians and activists on a weekly basis since the ceasefire had been signed. In September 2004 the number exceeded 250, according to the government. And the Norwegians have come under quite some criticism for not commenting publicly on these murders when they take place, and for continuing to deal with the LTTE in spite of them. The policy in Oslo has been to condemn 'killings in general' but avoid condemnation of individual murders.

Three days before Helgesen arrived in Colombo, members of the Tamil Eelam People's Democratic Party (EPDP) let the Norwegians know just how angry this policy made them. An enraged crowd of protestors brought the coffin carrying the body of Velayadun Ravindran, an EPDP activist who had been killed that week by the LTTE, and deposited it at the gates of the Norwegian embassy. It was a publicity stunt; but one which left many embassy staff shaken.

The killings aside, in a more general sense other Tamil political groups feel it is unjust that the Norwegians accept the LTTE's claim to be the 'sole representative' of Sri Lanka's Tamil community. In their defence, the Norwegians argue, it is not they who have accepted this, but the government. They agreed to this condition in the ceasefire agreement. 'If the government is willing to negotiate with the LTTE as the sole representative of the Tamil people, we are basically fine with that,' says Helgesen.

But there is a caveat: 'Our only principle is that of not excluding talking to anyone.' So on every trip Helgesen and Solheim make a point of seeing other Tamil leaders, as well as other political groups, including the leaders of the Muslim community, even though they are not part of the official process. Most prominent among them is the head of the EPDP, Douglas Devananda, who is a minister in the current government. He is so hated by the LTTE – a feeling that is mutual – that just two weeks before Helgesen arrived in July 2004, Devananda he was the apparent target of the first suicide bomb in the capital since 2001, which killed five people. News reports said the attack was a warning by the LTTE to Devananda and the government not to assist Karuna.

Just as the Norwegians do not see it as their role to get involved in the often murderous political dynamics of Sri Lanka, they also did not see it as their job to impose human rights standards in the actual ceasefire agreement. Helgesen is well aware of the criticism that the ceasefire agreement failed to spell out more specific human rights obligations. 'I understand that point. But I think such a process must be driven by the parties. And we shouldn't be too normative about what should be in it.'

In negotiating the ceasefire agreement, however, there were two issues they got involved in. The first was a commitment by both parties to banning land-mines. The second was to get the LTTE to give up the 'horrendous practice' of using child soldiers. At the time of the ceasefire the Tigers said they would stop it, but human rights groups since report that they never did.

For a country with a reputation as a passionate promoter of

human rights, the Norwegians take an unexpectedly agnostic approach to pushing a human rights agenda in the peace process. While working on the 'basic assumption that the biggest human rights violator is war', Helgesen says: 'We are not driving any agenda. We are not human rights advocates in the process, we are facilitators for both parties. We don't have a blueprint which we feel would be the best solution.'

The Norwegians hope they will nonetheless achieve the same outcome without having crossed the line from facilitator to advocate. 'We make it very clear to the parties that if economic development is going to take place, the international community is going to have do the funding, and it will not accept doing that unless human rights guarantees are in place.'

In their support for the Norwegian's peace process, some of the most prominent members of the international community are in a rather awkward position. This is because the LTTE is widely deemed to be a terrorist organization, and is proscribed in several countries, including the US, India, the UK, Canada, Malaysia and Australia.

Since the US launched its war on terror in the wake of 9/11, it has taken a far greater interest in dealing with terrorist organizations. While it was never involved in these negotiations, those close to the Norwegian's process say that none has been more supportive than the US. One source said they simply took the view that 'you just gotta deal with those bastards'. And how nice it was to have the Norwegians to do it for them.

In becoming facilitators for the peace process in Sri Lanka, the Norwegians were taking on a pariah insurgency group with whom none of their natural political allies could even, officially at least, have tea with. Once the ceasefire was established, this protocol eased. Donors had started making the long journey north in a bid to support the Norwegians in their efforts to keep the LTTE engaged in the process.

Not everyone was that keen on this slackening of the LTTE

proscription. Kumaratunga, whose party came back into government in April 2004, used her renewed political mandate to instruct the diplomatic community, in no uncertain terms, that all future visits to the rebel-held areas in the north would be frowned upon. They duly stopped, much to Helgesen's frustration.

During his visit in July 2004, Helgesen invited the diplomatic community over to lunch on Ambassador Brattskar's veranda. Under fans paddling noisily at the thick hot air, Helgesen stopped everyone mid-mouthful to make a request. Ambassadors the length of the table put their forks down to take notes. Having told them, like everyone else, 'we have a frozen war which is melting at the edges', he said the current isolation of the LTTE was not helping efforts to get them back to the negotiating table. 'Our genuine concern is that if pressure is to be put on the LTTE it has to be done by someone. And you are the obvious candidates.'

When the gaggle of ambassadors started eagerly reminding him that they had been banned from doing so, Helgesen told them that in his meeting with the President he had expressed his 'very strong disagreement' with this policy. He had told her: 'In our judgement, if the LTTE is to become part of the political mainstream they have to see people.' He then informed his lunch guests that in response to this, the government had relented and said that diplomats could go, providing they had a 'clear message and a reason to go'.

The EU found one. Disgusted by the recent behaviour of the LTTE, and with some of its members privately frustrated at the passivity of the Norwegians, it wanted to tell them off. In a sense, it was able to play bad cop to the Norwegians' softly, softly approach. Within a month an EU delegation visited Kilinochi, after which it released a strongly worded statement. On their killing of political opponents it declared 'there is no excuse for such violence'. It called the recruitment of child soldiers 'a breach of fundamental human rights' and warned the LTTE that compliance with human rights, good governance and democratic standards were necessary to the LTTE obtaining 'recognition as a political player in Sri Lanka'.

Since April 2003, despite repeated visits by Helgesen and Solheim and even the then Norwegian Foreign Minister, Jan Petersen, there has been little progress in getting the two sides back to the negotiating table. Even the $4.5 billion in aid pledged at a donors' conference in Tokyo in June 2003 has failed to act as a carrot to get either side to shift.

There was some hope that things might change in the aftermath of the tsunami in December 2004, which killed 30,000 people in Sri Lanka alone. It was assumed that in the wake of such a tragedy politicians on both sides might be moved to make concessions faster. Instead it turned out to be an opportunity to demonstrate just how intransigent each party could be. The hope of renewed peace talks soon fell off the agenda. It took six months for the two parties to even agree a deal on the distribution of humanitarian aid.

Helgesen strides through the Hilton's glittery lobby surrounded by his blond body guards, Sri Lankan police and his Norwegian entourage, en route to his final engagement with the President. The whirl of urgency with which he marches would make anyone watching think he was an important man with an important job on his hands. But no one is watching. The two Italian tourists dressed in shorts and t-shirts continue to pore over a map of Colombo with the concierge. At the patisserie counter in the lobby a family bicker over which cake to buy. In the bar beneath a huge chandelier businessmen are deep in deals over glasses of freshly squeezed mango juice and beer.

Downstairs in the immense ballroom, a high society wedding is taking place. Women radiating the pleasure of wealth are dressed in exquisite saris the shimmering hues of a tropical garden: emerald, magenta, vermillion, indigo. Hundreds of people have been invited. One of the guests, Sanjay, is seated at one of the many tables. He is a successful businessman in the garment industry. Like many from Sri Lanka's elite, he is not politically active. 'I don't vote. I don't believe in any of them. If these politicians really wanted peace, we would have peace. I am a Buddhist. And the first teaching of our Lord Buddha is that you don't kill.'

So the Buddhist monks in the parliament don't want peace? He raises his eyebrows. But what about the Norwegians, surely they want peace? He raises his eyebrows a little higher, his scepticism a perfect reflection of views widely expressed in the press. But unlike the media, Sanjay talks proudly of employing Tamils in his factory, and of having protected them during the 1983 attacks. With true Buddhist pragmatism, Sanjay accepts his country and his place in it, as it is. 'I have been born a Buddhist in this life, that is my Karma. Who knows what I will be in my next life? Maybe a Tamil.' He smiles at the thought of it. 'Or if I am unlucky, a Norwegian mediator.' And he laughs.

Postscript

Elections in 2005 in both Norway and Sri Lanka had an effect on the peace process in Sri Lanka. In November Mahinda Rajapakse took over the presidency from Kumaratunga on a hardline ticket which led many to doubt that the peace process and the Norwegians' role in it had a future. But against a backdrop of ever-spiralling violence, both sides eventually agreed to talk again. A change of government in Norway in September had led to, in good Norwegian fashion, Solheim and Helgesen more-or-less swapping places in the facilitation team. As head of the Norwegian delegation, Solheim who now held the post of Minister for International Development, oversaw a tentative round of new peace talks which began in Geneva in February 2006.

Selected sources

Reports and analysis

'Sri Lanka: Former Tamil Tiger Child Soldiers Remain at Risk', Human Rights Watch, 27 April 2004.

B Raman, 'The LTTE: The Metamorphosis', South Asia Analysis Group, 29 April 2002.

Dr S Chandrasekharan, 'Sri Lankan Peace Talks. What Next?', South Asia Analysis Group, 14 September 2002.

Dr S Chandrasekharan, 'Sri Lanka: Chandrika makes a tactical move', South Asia Analysis Group, 8 August 2004.

News sources

BBC News Online: Reports and Analysis.

'LTTE Protests "sidelining" of Solheim', *The Hindu*, 11 June 2001.

'The Facilitator Fracas', *Frontline*, 18(13), 23 June 2001.

'President Threatens to Cancel Ceasefire', *Tamilnet*, 26 February 2002.

'Editorial', *The Island*, 28 February 2002.

'Secretive Tamil Leader Speaks Out', *CNN*, 10 April 2002.

Alex Perry, 'Tamil Tiger Chief Emerges from the Shadows', *Time Asia*, 16 April 2002.

'US Backs Sri Lanka's Peace Process, Press Release', United States Consulate, Mumbai, India, 19 February 2003.

'Chronology of Sri Lanka's fragile peace bid', *AFP*, 22 April 2003.

Scott McDonald, 'Norway sees no peace role until Sri Lanka crisis ends', Reuters, 14 November 2003.

Edward Luce, 'Interview with Chandrika Kumaratunga', *Financial Times*, 17 November 2003.

'Sri Lanka's Parliament Reconvenes', *Associated Press*, 19 November 2003.

'Sri Lanka raises peace hopes despite killings', *AFP*, 5 September 2004.

'Sri Lanka: ceasefire still holds', *AFP*, 4 November 2004.

Other sources

www.slelections.gov.lk

5 The God-fearing General

Lazaro Sumbeiywo
Sudan

Born in 1947, Lt General Lazaro K Sumbeiywo (Rtd) trained at Britain's Sandhurst Royal Military Academy before joining the Kenyan Department of Defence. After stints in the Air Force, running military intelligence, and directing liaison in the President's Office, he became involved in the Somalia–Kenya Peace Initiative in 1996. In 2000 he was appointed head of the Kenyan Army. He still held this job in 2002, when he was made Kenya's Special Envoy to the Inter-Governmental Authority on Development (IGAD), a regional organization for the Horn of Africa. This position put him in charge of the organization's South Sudan peace process.

Beyond the funeral parlours, sewage works and roadside garden-stalls of Nairobi's periphery, and beyond that, through some scrubby forest and then down a long dirt-track, in October 2004 General Lazaro Sumbeiywo led a retreat. He had to escape the distractions of Kenya's capital, not for his sake – he would always choose the calm of his cattle farm over Nairobi – but he needed to get his negotiating teams away from the temptations of the city.

Sumbeiywo, although now retired, sounds like he is still in uniform. The click-click of his brogues march across the court-yard at a pace that would leave most breathless. The buzz and luxury of the Intercontinental Hotel in Nairobi, where this round of South Sudan peace talks began a few days before, has been replaced with the austere accommodation of Kenya Commercial Bank's training centre, in the district of Karen. The three postwar blocks, set around a circular courtyard, look like a military academy. No wonder Sumbeiywo feels at home here. Not so the negotiating teams. 'The parties call this place the "open prison",' says Sumbeiywo, a gruff grin spreading across his face. As he explains: 'They can leave if they want, but there is no where to go to, if they do.'

Sumbeiywo had commanded this leg of the South Sudan Peace process for nearly three years now. In 21 years of conflict between the Sudanese government and the rebel Southern Sudan People's Liberation Movement/Army (SPLM/A) as many as two million people had died, and millions more had been forced to flee their homes. Sumbeiywo was appointed to the job in 2002, not because he was a professional mediator, but because, as head of the Kenyan army, he was a trusted confidante of President Daniel arap Moi, in whose gift the chief mediator's position fell. But his involvement in the mediation, which was run by the IGAD, a regional organization for the Horn of Africa, went back much further.

IGAD's mediation had started well in 1994 with a Declaration of Principles being signed within the year. Although the process then dragged on in fits and starts throughout the 1990s, this document had established two main principles which would remain at the heart of the agreement finally signed in January 2005. Firstly, both parties would seek to retain the unity of the country by creating a state which respected the rights of all its people, and secondly, should it fail to do this, the people of South Sudan would have the right to self-determination through a referendum, leading, if so desired, to independence.

Sumbeiywo had inadvertently become involved in the talks at this early stage when he was head of military intelligence. By the early 1990s, because of this work, Sumbeiywo already had established contacts in the SPLM/A leadership. So when in 1994 the parties were in need of a venue for their talks, he gave them office space. And from there, he says simply, 'I got interested in the process.' By 1997 he had been appointed Kenya's Special Envoy to the IGAD process, a position which automatically put him in charge. As the only one of the six other IGAD states to have reasonable relations with both the Khartoum government and the SPLM/A, Kenya was the obvious candidate to lead a South Sudan peace process.

Kenya had long been affected by the South Sudan conflict. During the course of the fighting, millions of South Sudanese refugees had spilled across Kenya's northern border and Kenya had found itself playing host to one of the world's longest running multi-billion dollar international aid operations.

The other IGAD members participating in the mediation – who also share borders with Sudan: Eritrea, Ethiopia, and Uganda – had all been involved in providing support to one side or the other at various stages in the war. IGAD, whose members comprise a complex web of historical rivalries and shifting political alliances, has a mandate for regional security. With internal unrest ongoing in practically every member state, resolving the conflict in South Sudan, in which nearly every country was in some way involved, was deemed to be in everyone's interest.

Despite the US, when it became involved in 2002, referring to the IGAD process simply as a Kenyan one, in principle it was a team game. At least Sumbeiywo and the other IGAD members considered it so. He says he constantly used the other IGAD envoys from Uganda, Eritrea, Ethiopia and Djibouti, whom he referred to as 'my ambassadors', to push and prod the process, exploiting their particular political leanings (for example, Ethiopia's with the Sudanese government and Uganda's with the SPLM/A) as necessary. One of these ambassadors says Sumbeiywo was inclusive in his approach. 'Even though he is a military man, he is not a dictator. He consults us, and wants to hear our ideas. We feel we are members of one family.'

In 1997 the parties signed another Declaration of Principles which mapped out in more detail the basis for the 2005 peace agreement. It reiterated the right of southerners to self-determination through a referendum with the understanding that national unity remained the priority. It also stipulated the need to establish a secular state, a system of governance based on multi-party democracy, decentralization through a federal system and respect for human rights.

In the following two years little progress was made in pushing the mediation beyond these principles, and in 1999 Sumbeiywo went off to the Royal College of Defence to examine in theory some of those issues he couldn't resolve in practice. He wrote his thesis on 'The Dilemma of the Horn of Africa'. His conclusion for Sudan was that the problem was solvable but that 'the government was in denial and they would one day accept this fact'.

US involvement and the 'observers'

The Sudanese government did come to this point of realization. But it was not a voluntary process. Since its backing for Saddam Hussein's regime in Iraq during the 1990–91 Gulf War, the US had set itself against the regime of President Al-Bashir who seized power in a coup in 1989. In the mid-1990s Sudan had been found to be sheltering Osama bin Laden. Because of this association with Bin Laden, in 1998 the Clinton Administration bombed a pharmaceutical factory on the edge of Khartoum. It was revenge for the bombing of US embassies in Nairobi and Dar-es-Salaam a few months earlier which bin Laden was believed to have masterminded.

This bombing, which at the time Washington claimed was targeting a chemical weapons factory, left its mark on the Khartoum regime. The Sudanese government was further unnerved by the US military campaign to unseat the Taliban in Afghanistan following the September 11 attacks. President Bush's determination to deal with what it termed 'rogue regimes' was evident. The possibility that it could be next on the White House's list quietly hounded the Sudanese government through three years of mediation and into finally putting its signature on a peace accord.

The aggressive resolve of the United States' war on terrorism was not, in fact, the original source of its uncommon involvement to spearhead an end to conflict in Africa. The Bush

Administration's interest in the South Sudan war actually predated the 9/11 attacks and was a result of domestic pressure, not foreign policy. It came in the form of a law which committed the government to find a peace deal in South Sudan.

Attempts to pass what became known as the Sudan Peace Act (SPA) through Congress had rumbled on throughout Bush's first term in office. It was eventually passed in 2002. This unusual law, which committed the US to pressuring Khartoum to end the war in South Sudan, was the result of a curious alliance between two factions in Congress. On one side the anti-slavery lobby, led by the Congressional Black Caucus, was fighting to stop the continuing practice of southerners being taken into slavery by government-backed militia. On the other, Bush's own Evangelical Christian lobby wanted to prevent the continued persecution by the Islamist government of their 'brothers' in South Sudan (most southerners are non-Muslim). The signing of the SPA was marked by a ceremony in which President Bush was presented with a burnt Bible found in the home of a Christian family who had been attacked in the south. On giving it to him, one activist asked the President to 'pray for our persecuted brethren in Sudan'. Bush responded by saying: 'Thank you, I will.'

President Bush responded to the SPA by appointing former Senator John Danforth as his special envoy for peace in South Sudan. His initial mandate was to report on whether the parties were ready for peace. This report, which came out in April 2002, conveyed with unblushing clarity the Evangelist lobby's own particular understanding of the conflict. Danforth wrote of how he said he had spoken to many southerners who were 'struggling to hold to their faith in the face of privation and attack'. He said one of his most memorable experiences had been in an open air Episcopal service near a bombed out church in the south. 'The faith of the congregation was something I will always treasure,' he wrote. In his consultations in Europe, he visited not only countries with an interest in the conflict such as Britain, Norway and Italy, but also the Vatican and the Archbishop of Canterbury, to discuss the 'religious situation'. Danforth's analysis laid out a clear conflict between Islam and Christianity. Danforth acknowledged that it might be more complicated than this when he admitted: 'a number of people told me that their sense of being persecuted involves race, ethnicity and culture', but he did not sound convinced as he finished this sentence with the words: 'but it clearly involves religion'. While most southerners are not Muslim, they are not necessarily Christian, a fact not mentioned in the report.

Danforth concluded that the US could most usefully push the cause of peace by helping to 'harmonize' existing initiatives. The Sudanese government had long used the tactic of having more than one mediation on the go at a time in order to dilute any real effort to resolve the conflict. And so Danforth was referring to both an Egyptian-Libyan mediation proposal being floated at the time, as well as IGAD's ongoing efforts.

But it ended up being IGAD's long-standing efforts which the US would work through to get a peace deal. Until the US got involved, the eight-year-old IGAD mediation had never managed to move the process beyond a Declaration of Principles. Now the US, with the support of three other nations, Britain, Norway and, to a lesser extent, Italy, formed a quartet of 'observers' to the IGAD mediation, more commonly known as the Troika because of Italy's minor role. It provided, in effect, the engine needed to push the process forward.

The use of the term 'observer' allowed the revamped IGAD process to technically remain a regional affair. But the US was now aiming to drive its own agenda through the process, and this became a repeated cause of contention between Sumbeiywo and the observers. Danforth had argued in his report that 'any peace negotiation must address the relationship between religion and government, frankly and at length, perhaps with the mediation of Muslim and Christian leaders from outside Sudan'. This religious bent ignored the wealth and power issues driving the conflict. It was no coincidence that the war had started only five years after oil was discovered in the south of the country. As far as the

SPLM/A's peace agenda was concerned, its leader, John Garang, was known during the negotiations not for his enthusiasm for religious freedom so much as the chance an agreement would provide for establishing the political rights of the southern Sudanese. An agreement would also make him Vice-President of the largest country in Africa. On 9 July 2005, after more than two decades of fighting, he achieved this. Three weeks later he was killed when the helicopter he was travelling in, which belonged to President Museveni of Uganda, crashed, apparently as a result of bad weather.

In order to maintain their influence, the observers constantly tried to keep tabs on the proposals coming out of the talks. Some members of the IGAD Secretariat say they repeatedly came under pressure from diplomats from observer countries to give them documents which Sumbeiywo wanted to keep confidential. Despite this, Sumbeiywo readily admits that the mediation could not have succeeded without the support of the observers, particularly the US. But from his point of view he was running a regional process. His aim was always to produce a Sudanese solution, not necessarily based on highly idealized principles of rights and freedoms but based on his pragmatic motto of 'it's not what you want, it's what you can live with'.

The attempts of the US to inflect the agreement with its own sense of Christian-infused moral righteousness repeatedly riled Sumbeiywo – who, himself, has an exceptionally strong Christian faith. He did what he could to protect the process from what he considered as outside interference. This drove Sumbeiywo, on more than one occasion, to threaten to shoot the US envoy to the talks. On other occasions, when US pressure to manipulate the process got too much, he offered to resign and let the US take over. But in what proved to be a co-dependent relationship, it never took up his offer.

Sumbeiywo's approach

Sumbeiywo's unflinching self-confidence, his military manner, his handsome height and his high, proud cheek bones make him quite an intimidating figure; something exacerbated by him not being a man impressed by rank. He talks with a husky weariness, which after nearly three years of intense mediation borders on contempt, about nearly everyone he has had to deal with, be they government ministers, ambassadors or senior international dignitaries. The parties themselves weathered Sumbeiywo's lack of deference, not least because, as head of the Kenyan army, his military background commanded a great deal of respect. Unlike many mediators, he understood the psychology of war and they trusted him because of this. It was this trust which he says was vital in helping change the militarized mind-sets of the parties. 'You can bring in all the new structures you like, but if you don't have a change of attitude then you will achieve nothing. The war will continue.'

While Sumbeiywo does not have a formal background in international diplomacy, unlike any other mediator in this book he can claim to have the art of conflict resolution in his blood. His father was a chief in the town of Iten in the Great Rift Valley and part of his job was settling disputes within the tribe. Such was his knack for doing this that he ended up as chairman of the African Tribunal Court. 'He used to settle a lot of conflict. I learnt a lot from him, not from formal teaching so much as simply watching him at work,' Sumbeiywo says.

Despite this, Sumbeiywo's lifelong career in the army meant that there were many aspects of the South Sudan mediation which he was not at ease dealing with alone. He admits, for example, he felt more at home with the security issues than resolving the political questions. Because of this, he brought in two experts to run the process which he, in a presidential way, oversaw. Nicholas Haysom, a South African constitutional lawyer, had worked closely for Nelson Mandela for many years. Julian Hottinger, who comes from the Swiss Federal Department of Foreign Affairs, is an international and linguistic chameleon, fluent in several languages; after four years working on the Northern Ireland peace process he speaks English like a native of Belfast. Between them, they have a vast range of experience in peace processes which includes South Africa, Somalia, Burundi, Rwanda, Nepal, the Basque region, Vietnam, Sri Lanka and Nigeria. They have frequently worked closely together and joke about their sales pitch which runs: 'Haysom and Hottinger, no conflict too big, no fight too small, we solve them all.'

The Machakos talks, May 2002

In May 2002 Sumbeiywo began a new round of peace talks which, invigorated by the new international enthusiasm for success, were aimed at producing sustained rather than sporadic negotiations. The process began by committing the two parties to an intense six-week stint of negotiations in the Kenyan town of Machakos.

Things got off to a ropey start with Sumbeiywo clashing with the Sudanese government. As Ahmed Derdiery, deputy head of the Sudanese government's mission in Nairobi, says of these early stages of the talks, 'Our toughest sessions for quite some time were with Sumbeiywo rather than the SPLM/A.' In preparatory meetings for the Machakos session, the talks had fallen into difficulty, with the government refusing to sign a modalities paper on how the process would be run. This infuriated Sumbeiywo, who treated such behaviour not as political manoeuvring but as blatant insubordination. Sumbeiywo had made it clear the negotiations would be based on the 1997 Declaration of Principles, which the government wanted to renegotiate. In the first of many instances, he lost his temper. 'The General threatened to tell the international community that the government of Sudan was reneging on the process,' says one of the senior negotiators for the Sudanese government. The government's reaction forced Sumbeiywo to start rethinking his own approach when its delegation simply gathered its papers and walked out. 'The next day he found most of us were already back in Khartoum,' the negotiator says, adding: 'He learnt to do things differently after this.'

Learning, listening and changing tactics is how those around Sumbeiywo frequently describe the way he works. They say he grew into the art of mediation on the job. Dr Cirino Hiteng, one of the SPLM/A negotiators, who has known him for many years, says Sumbeiywo adapted to his new role: 'He has really evolved from a soldier to a diplomat. The process has taught him a lot.'

The Machakos talks began with the parties presenting their own papers on the key issues in the Declaration of Principles. The aim of the following six weeks was to compile these ideas into a single negotiating text from which to work. In order to provide the parties with a starting point, over the course of a night the IGAD mediators and some of the observers sat together in the IGAD office and produced a first draft. This covered broad outlines on main issues, including, the transition period, the pre-transition period, the need for a process of reconciliation, and the equitable sharing of natural resources. It did not, however, specifically refer to the right to self-determination, nor did it refer to the 'right to secede'. It was a mistake which left not just one of the parties, but the mediation's key backer, furious.

On receiving the draft document the SPLM/A went 'ballistic', says one of the IGAD staff. Not only the SPLM/A – the US envoy to the process 'just snapped. He swore, went red in the face and walked out.' Such a document put the US in an awkward position. 'The US had been promising the SPLM/A certain things that, because it was not in charge of the process, it simply was not in a position to guarantee,' said the member of the IGAD team.

Sumbeiywo and the observers

Sumbeiywo's relationship with the observers, particularly the US, was fraught at many points. Although he accepts that 'any mediator worth his salt should understand he does not have a sole monopoly on the process', he did consider it a process of which he was in command. 'I lead the process. Sometimes I disagree with people, people who want to take over from me. But I refuse to let them. I need to have everybody on board and everybody must listen to me. I will listen to them but the final word is mine.'

Such a claim would probably cause many a diplomatic eyebrow to rise. But there is a distinct disjuncture between the process which Sumbeiywo saw himself as leading, and the one which the observer powers consider they forced along. For most mediators, their backers – those international powers who provide political and moral, as well as financial, support for a mediation process – are the people a mediator most relies on. Not Sumbeiywo. He describes himself as the 'manager of a fragile coalition' in which he was piggy in the middle.

For him, both the observers and the regional powers of IGAD were all partial players, trying to shape the outcome of the process. Hence, he says, with a disillusioned rasp in his voice: 'I have learnt there are no friends, there are only interests.'

'I sit in the middle and the parties and the observers form a circle around me. Their interests change whereas mine don't.' How does he define his interest? 'My interest is peace in the Sudan. Their interest is who has the upper hand when they get peace in the Sudan.

'The US, for example, is an "interest" in that it is currently the main supporter of the process.' Sumbeiywo says it is he who decides when to use these 'interests' to push the process forward. 'You've got to be able to pick and choose which pressure or inducement will make the parties move. If my interest is for the Americans to support me in something, that interest takes precedence over everything else.'

The tensions in the process were deep. Even how to define 'peace in Sudan' remained a source of contention throughout. 'I am not creating a "New Sudan". That is why I disagree with some of the other interests who want to create a "New Sudan". I am interested in peace between the north and south. That is my mandate, and I am sticking to it.'

The Machakos process was got back on track through a series of workshops which got the parties examining the very emotive subjects contained in the Declaration of Principles, namely, self-determination, and the issue of state and religion.

The early workshops in Machakos sound more like rounds of group therapy than hard-nosed political discussions. One of the Haysom/Hottinger techniques is to get the parties to vent their feelings, thrashing out their understanding of the political issues they have to negotiate before actually getting down to debating the detail. After 20 years of civil war and two million people dead, those feelings ran deep.

In a series of workshops and plenary sessions in which responses were scribbled onto large pieces of paper sellotaped to the walls around the room, the negotiators responded to questions like: 'What does slavery mean to you?', 'What does it mean to be African? Or Arab?', 'What do you understand by self-determination?', 'What do you understand by religious freedom?'

'Some of it was really quite uncomfortable,' remembers Susan Page, the legal advisor to the IGAD Secretariat. Some in the SPLM/A questioned whether government officials who happened to be black, could really define themselves as Arab. Government officials tried to 'play down' the government's own culpability for the continuation of slavery by saying their grandparents had suffered from it too. One SPLM/A commander, whose former university classmates were sitting in the room on the government side, talked about the humiliation of having to change his name to Ahmed when he was in Khartoum. When it came to religious freedoms, government officials defended existing rules by saying there was nothing stopping Christians building churches in the north, for example. The SPLM/A responded that you needed a permit to do this, and permits, for one reason or another, were never granted for such things.

Some would say that this kind of technique, where the parties play out in public the role of the oppressed and the oppressor, was simply 'theatre' for the Western mediators and observers. After all, the relationship between these negotiators is more complex than that of victim and abuser. In some sense many members of the negotiating team are part of the same Sudanese elite. Many of them knew each other long before the negotiation started; several of them went to university together; some are even related. Others have even crossed over from one side to another and back again. So while religion and racism may be dominating factors in the South Sudan conflict, after two decades of war these negotiations were really not so much about issues of right and wrong, as control of wealth and power. Nonetheless, Sumbeiywo says this process of 'ventilation' was vital in getting a change in attitude, particularly among the government negotiators. 'They had to come to a point where they realized that the path of marginalization was not worth pursuing. This was a fundamental change.

'We did this by allowing them to talk to each other, and ventilating. Allowing them to ventilate completely and allowing them to say everything they wanted to say.'

Out of these tough debates three documents were drawn up on Self-Determination, State and Religion, and a Religious 'bill of rights'. Susan Page, who was the drafter for this process, says that there were intense debates over every line of the text, and sometimes over each word. One of the difficulties she faced was over translation. Some key words, for example, like 'sovereignty', do not translate easily from English into Arabic. 'I was accused of all sorts of things because of this,' says Page. 'But it did come from both sides, and it was because people were having to make difficult choices.'

Unable to resolve these choices in the larger working groups, Sumbeiywo took matters in hand. On 17 July 2002, three days before the talks were due to end, Sumbeiywo, with exquisite military efficiency, decided things needed to be speeded up. He put the two most senior negotiators from each side into a room with an ashtray for the government's chain-smoking Said Katib, let them keep their mobile phones and gave them plentiful supplies of tea. Closing the door behind him, he told them: 'I am giving you one hour.'

'The General made it very clear that you can change the text as you like, as long as you both agree. We are not going to change it unilaterally,' says Page. After one hour, Sumbeiywo returned and the two sides asked for one more hour.

After two hours they'd come up with their changes on the three documents. 'And we celebrated,' laughs Page.

The parties continued to nit-pick over various clauses even as the press were gathered to cover the signing of what became the Machakos protocols. But in the end they put their signatures to 'most of the documents'. In doing so they committed themselves to self-determination for the south; the right of the government to have Shar'ia Law in the north, and a framework for future negotiations.

In drawing up this framework for negotiations, Sumbeiywo had given into the SPLM/A desire to talk without first establishing a ceasefire. At this stage he was prepared to go along with the notion that the pressure of war would actually help push the process forward. Moreover, the theory goes, it should prevent the frozen status quo of the battlefield being interpreted into an unjust agreement at the negotiating table. But despite the signing of the Machakos protocols and a first meeting between the Sudanese President Al Bashir and John Garang, the SPLM/A leader, in the summer of 2002, the fighting in the south did not stop. In September, the government of Sudan pulled out of the peace talks after the SPLM/A captured the strategically important town of Torit. This led to an intensive military response by government forces which reclaimed the town less than a month later.

The experience of the government walk-out changed Sumbeiywo's mind about the need for a ceasefire. 'It's not good to have reports from the field listing the number of people killed coming through to the negotiating table where the two sides are trying to make peace. It's not practical.'

So in October 2002 a ceasefire was agreed which would last the duration of the talks. And although fighting continued sporadically throughout the talks, 'It held, not more or less, but more than less,' says Sumbeiywo.

Dr Mutrif Siddig, the Sudanese Deputy Minister of Foreign Affairs, says that Sumbeiywo deftly got the two parties talking again by making full use of the observers. 'This was one of the critical times he managed to bring the parties back into the process. He spread his wings, and in this case his wings were the observers, who played a crucial role. It was they who could apply pressure and incentives by talking about a peace dividend.'

Sumbeiywo had his own access to lines of official influence and power. He had worked closely with Kenyan President Daniel arap Moi for more than a decade. The parties say they found Sumbeiywo's relationship with Moi useful for the process. But being one of Moi's men nearly cost him his job in December 2002 when, after 24 years of rule, Moi lost the elections in December 2002. Sumbeiywo was replaced as the head of the Kenyan army, a job he had managed until then to combine with the mediation process. The new regime under President Mwai Kibaki also talked of replacing him as the mediator. It took the parties to step in and insist that he stay. 'The parties helped convince the new government to keep him,' says one of the government negotiators. 'By this time he had the confidence of both the parties and the international community and we wanted him to stay in the process.'

Earlier on in the negotiations, however, Sumbeiywo's perceived closeness to Moi had been used against him by the government when some of its negotiators, alluding to the well-known scandals which followed the Moi regime throughout its lengthy rule, accused Sumbeiywo of corruption. 'He angrily challenged them to prove it,' says one of the IGAD staff, and then stormed out of the room. It's not surprising he took offence. His nickname when he was head of the army was 'Zulu Tango' – which stood for Zero Tolerance, the anti-corruption campaign he led when Moi appointed him as head of the army. Colonel

Jonathan Krop, one of his colleagues in the army, said when he took the job in 2000, 'There were a lot of problems at that time. People were not returning stores, money was not accounted for, bills were unpaid. Also there was a huge backlog of discipline cases which were still to be dealt with.' Sumbeiywo launched his campaign within months of taking control of the army. 'He stood firm,' says Krop. 'It took a lot of courage. He sacked many people, even from his generation, even his peers, even brigadiers, even people from his own tribe.'

Sumbeiywo's eldest daughter, Flora, says it was a low-profile campaign. 'He stood in the way of a lot of people. He did so very firmly. But it was never announced. He did it subtly, people were just seen to retire.'

It was an obvious jibe for the Sudanese government to have made, inferring as it did that Sumbeiywo was somehow tainted through his association with the corruption of the Moi regime. But Flora, who has the same regal self-possession as her father, says his relationship to Moi was simply one of professional loyalty: 'He just worked for him.'

Nakuru, July 2003
Over the course of the year following the signing of the Machakos protocol, the talks which at this time were dealing with each issue sequentially, made no progress. Even though in Machakos many of the basic principles had been worked out, there were still huge areas where nothing was agreed. These included deals on power sharing, wealth sharing and the three contested areas of Abyei, the Nuba Mountains and the Southern Blue Nile.

So Sumbeiywo and his team decided to try a new approach at the round of talks which took place at the Sarova Lion Hill Lodge in Nakuru in July 2003. They would present the parties with a comprehensive document designed to allow them to trade issues off one another and by doing so hopefully push the process forward. 'By the time of the Nakuru document it was clear that the guys whom we were negotiating with were not willing to take decisions,' says Hottinger. They worked on the assumption that if the document were rejected it would allow the mediators to say, 'We are in crisis, we can't go forward, we have to take the negotiations to a higher level.'

'For a whole year we had been going round and round in circles,' adds Haysom, who says he knew at the time that presenting the parties with a ready-made draft of a comprehensive document was a high-risk strategy. He was right. It backfired.

The Sudanese government was furious. 'When you put a document like this on the table you expect a riot. You always try to dissatisfy both sides. That's important,' says Hottinger. 'That way they are both unhappy and have something in common.'

But the parties reacted very differently, Haysom says. 'The government said the document was biased in favour of the SPLM/A. This wasn't helped by the SPLM/A saying it was an "excellent compromise",' says Haysom.

The ICG argued at the time that 'on the whole the proposals were fair'. The mediators had prioritized keeping Sudan a single state by making attractive proposals on power and wealth sharing to the south. But the government, because it already had a monopoly on both Sudan's power and wealth, found it hard to accept the serious compromises that getting a peace deal would involve on its part. In terms of the actual give and take of the agreement, it would mean, on the face of it, it had to give more than it would gain.

Prior to the Nakuru document they had dealt with each contentious issue separately. 'Until now we had allowed them to swallow the elephant bite by bite,' says Haysom, remarking the comprehensive nature of the Nakuru document was a shock for the government. 'It was a reality sandwich which was too much for them to swallow at once.'

They didn't even try. President Bashir announced the IGAD mediators could 'soak the [Nakuru] draft in water, drink the ink and go to hell', and demanded that Sumbeiywo be removed from the process. The Sudanese government then started nosing about for alternative mediators, looking at options in the African Union, the Arab League and with Egypt.

The issue that had pushed the government over the edge was the notion of a 'Shari'a-free' Khartoum. This reflected American thinking which wanted to assert the principle of equality of religion and freedom of expression. Someone close to the process says that the mediators came under heavy pressure from the US and the Norwegians to 'guarantee Garang a Shari'a-free Khartoum'. But the government angrily responded that such a proposal was backtracking on the Machakos protocols which accepted that the north would be run under Shari'a law.

It was a pivotal moment in the process. The observers' drive to meet the demands of their own political constituencies back home – by breaking the hegemony of Shari'a rule in the capital – had tipped the process against the interests of the parties. Sumbeiywo saw this and in the midst of the breakdown of the process he threatened to shoot the American envoy, Jeff Millington, and then threw him out of his office.

Sumbeiywo is famous for his quick temper, which has affected almost everyone involved in the process. With exceptional understatement, Dr Cirino Hiteng from the SPLM/A says: 'Sometimes he is very frank. Occasionally he gets very agitated. But that's the best way. It's all done in public.'

Sumbeiywo says that in part it comes from the army tradition of being straight with people. 'As a military man I deal with each party firmly. If they are wrong, I tell them that they are wrong. I do not mince my words.'

Even though mincing words is what peace mediators, desperate not to upset their delicate process, usually do, Haysom believes that Sumbeiywo's temper was actually an asset in the mediation. 'Often in mediations, if people are too emotionally in control it almost raises a suspicion of perhaps being calculating or cunning whereas the General's transparency has helped in creating a sense of trust. He has never lost his temper with just one person or just one side. It was seen almost as evidence of his emotional transparency, his fairness, in a sense. He'll lose it if pushed from whatever direction. When he loses his temper it doesn't matter who he loses it with, it can be an ambassador, a minister, or one of the parties. In effect his temper has helped protect the process from outside interference.'

When asked about the incident with the American ambassador, Sumbeiywo laughs. 'But I have thrown many, many ambassadors out of my office,' he says with a broad smile and a twinkle in his eye. But isn't he afraid about the repercussions of such undiplomatic behaviour? Without hesitation he responds: 'I fear no one but God.'

Sumbeiywo and God

This was evidently a bit of a problem for the observers, even Bush's supposedly Evangelical envoys, because it is true. And it meant that however strong the leverage the observers had over the parties, they had little over Sumbeiywo. With the US in particular, when it came to the crunch, and they could not agree, Sumbeiywo would simply offer to resign, and let them take over. 'Threatening to walk out, it's as if to say: "You need me, as much as I need you",' says one of the IGAD team, who watched it happen repeatedly over the course of the mediation.

That Sumbeiywo would threaten to quit the process is quite believable. He talks about his job with conviction, but unlike other mediators, there's no passion. Asked if he would go on to do further conflict resolution, he replies: 'If people want me to do it I will do it. But I will not seek it out because there is no enjoyment in it, I can assure you that. It's taxing.'

Sumbeiywo admits that he was confounded at times when the process was stuck. 'When the parties are in deadlock, and you want to tell the world that you are stuck, you can't, and you just have to find a way out. It's like being a surgeon with a patient who has a tumour. You can simply sew him back up, but the patient might die. Or you can cut out the tumour, but even then the patient might die. So do you cut or do you sew?'

Ask Sumbeiywo what keeps him going and he says: 'You have to have faith in what you are doing. And you've got to trust in God. You've got to listen to the voice of God.' When Sumbeiywo had a problem with the parties and the process was stuck, he didn't turn to the observers, he turned to prayer. 'I would just go away, from the talks, my own staff, from myself. And I would think about it and pray. And go as God led me.' Sometimes this was to his cattle farm in the Rift Valley or to his church in Nairobi where he'd find his pastor the Reverend Matthews Mwalw'a. 'Sometimes he'd just walk in here and you could tell from his face that he needed help. He'd say simply: "Things are not good, just pray",' says Mwalw'a.

Sumbeiywo, who is an elder in the Africa Inland Church in Nairobi, would brief the congregation every Sunday on progress in the talks. On occasion he even gave a copy of the agenda for the ongoing negotiations to the priests and elders of the church so they knew what time they should be praying for the process. At times, the involvement of the congregation got quite detailed with Sumbeiywo asking specific priests and elders to focus their prayers on different issues or certain individuals in the negotiation who were seen to be holding up progress. During the tense negotiations leading to the signing of the power-sharing protocols in May 2004, with Sumbeiywo stuck in the talks, his wife, Lorna, represented him in a prayer group focusing on a breakthrough. 'That week was very intense,' says Mwalw'a, 'not just for the General but for us as well.'

His wife Lorna, a gentle, elegant woman who runs a fabric import business, supported her husband throughout the mediation, tolerating week after week of his absence without complaint. She says simply: 'I think it's his calling. Everyone has a vocation for something. This is his.'

Naivasha, September 2003
In August 2003, after much prodding by the observers, a further round of talks were held in the Kenyan town of Nanyuki. But no

progress was made. The SPLM/A was wanting to negotiate on the basis of the Nakuru document, which the government refused to do.

With the process in crisis, some in the IGAD Secretariat say it was the pressure the regional powers put on the parties which initially broke the deadlock. 'The donors are, of course, always the ones claiming credit,' says Page. 'But at that point IGAD asserted itself. It was the presidents of the region who got it back on track.'

The Kenyans offered to host a summit between John Garang and Vice-President Taha. Over the previous year Garang had, for the first time, met on two occasions with the Sudanese President Al Bashir. But now it wasn't just a meeting but a negotiation which was being suggested, and the SPLM/A was hesitant. If high-level negotiations failed, it was felt a return to war was the only option open to them, something which many in the military wing of the organization were already pushing for. Vice-President Taha, on the other hand, saw it as a path which would enable his own political ascendancy, and was keen for the meeting to go ahead. With no other options on the table, it actually took the observers to wade in and persuaded Garang to agree to talk directly to Taha. In September 2003, in the Kenyan town of Naivasha, this high-level negotiation began.

This meeting transformed the nature of the mediation. The observers no longer sat in on the talks, the IGAD Secretariat also pulled out, and with it, Sumbeiywo. No non-Sudanese were present in the actual talks which three weeks later produced an agreement on security arrangements. This included the government agreeing to withdraw 80 per cent of its soldiers from the south; the two sides retaining their own armies during the six-year period leading to the referendum; and the deployment of a joint force made up of 20,000 soldiers in areas of continued conflict.

Some of the observers say that Sumbeiywo was no longer so important once the Naivasha talks got under way, as the process had moved to the highest diplomatic and political level. 'His most important role was during the first year, after that he was more of a facilitator. In Naivasha the principals worked it out themselves, conferring with the observers as needed,' said a senior Norwegian official; although one of IGAD team notes that actually Sumbeiwyo was never completely out of the picture: 'No deal was ever closed in any of the protocols, without Sumbeiywo's intervention, at some point.'

The observers may stress Sumbeiywo's diminished role at this stage of the negotiation but the parties themselves do not. At the Naivasha talks Sumbeiywo, along with his team, sat on the side lines, helping with technical arrangements and offering advice and support when wanted. 'It was no less important than what he had been doing before,' says Mutrif. 'In fact, it was as valuable as when he was doing the direct mediation.' Derdiery agrees: 'We really appreciated that at this point the General stepped aside. The fact that he was prepared to step out and be overshadowed by these two big leaders was so important. Many mediators would not have been happy to do this. It took real courage to step out of the limelight and be overshadowed.'

His own exclusion from this part of the process echoed a message he had long been giving the parties. 'He recognized that no one could resolve it better than us,' says Mutrif. 'He said: "I will facilitate and prepare the ground for you but you must analyse, discuss and come up with the solutions."'

The evident trust the parties ended up having in Sumbeiywo emerged over the course of the negotiations despite the recurrent set-backs. This is particularly true of the government side which had begun the process quite wary of him. 'Even after we were very upset about the Nakuru document and we criticized him personally, he did not take offence,' says Ahmed Derdiery. 'One of his major achievements is the way both parties view him,' says Hiteng. 'I think they both see him as fair.'

Even the government which had been pushing for his removal after the Nakuru document was issued, came to appreciate Sumbeiywo's defence of the parties against outside interests. 'As a government we are highly indebted to his integrity even if very often we have fallen out. He protects us from the international community. He knows our interests better than them. And he feels uncomfortable when outsiders try to move in,' adds Derdiery.

Those outsiders were seen to 'try to move in' in the October round of peace talks between Taha and Garang which began dealing with wealth and power sharing and the control of the three disputed areas. A week into the talks, the US Secretary of State Colin Powell visited the talks in Naivasha. The BBC reported that he came away saying he had a 'promise from the leaders to conclude a final deal by the end of December'. A government spokesman rebuked this, saying: 'It is impossible for anyone to dictate a date on the two parties that are negotiating.' US officials were adamant the deadline would be met and were saying the two parties would then be invited to the US for a signing ceremony on the White House lawn. Those close to Sumbeiywo say he told Colin Powell he would refuse to let this happen. It was, after all, a Kenyan-led process and any ceremony would take place in Nairobi. One of the mediators says the US agenda was clear: 'They were putting pressure on the parties because they wanted to claim success in the peace process in time for State of the Union Address in January 2004.'

Despite the recurrent tensions between the US and Sumbeiywo, the General was the first to acknowledge that without US backing the mediation would not have been successful. What's more, his inner circle say that he valued the personal support he received from Colin Powell and worried about losing it should he step down as Secretary of State. In the autumn of 2004, Sumbeiywo admitted he was concerned that should Bush lose the US election, the change in the team supporting the process might adversely affect it. By then the final signing was tantalizingly close. The two sides had agreed to the power-and wealth-sharing protocol, signed in May 2004, and were working at a technical level on the implementation details of the agreement.

Darfur

In the months leading up to these technical talks which begun in October 2004, the focus of the diplomatic community had shifted away from resolving the conflict in the south of the country. Attention had turned instead to the horrors which had been taking place in the western province of Darfur where over 16 months pro-government militia had intensified attacks on the civilian population in what had begun as a response to an insurgency. At least 180,000 people had died and more than two million people been displaced. In the summer of 2004, as the mediation entered its final phase, the issue of Darfur began to dominate the international headlines. And as US and European leaders responded with pledges to resolve the situation, Sumbeiywo felt the international resolve to push through the agreement for the South of the country, wilt. 'I was abandoned by the international community.' He even went off to Khartoum to ask them to 'come back'. 'They said: "No, give us time to stabilize Darfur and then we will come back".'

Sumbeiywo believes that downgrading the South Sudan process at that point was potentially counter-productive because, he argues, the peace agreement would help establish a model which could be used in other parts of the country. 'If the agreement is properly implemented it will resolve the other conflicts in Sudan. The agreement means there is somebody else joining the government in the centre which in turn means the government will not be able to continue marginalizing other areas of the country as it has done in the past.'

But did he not think that the SPLM/A would be given a disproportionate amount of power once it held the position of Vice-President, compared to other factions in the country? 'In this negotiation there is inclusivity. We have attempted to include other people in the south and the north so it is not a monopoly of the SPLM/A and the government. After three years, all the parties will get the chance to compete for power through the electoral process.'

Haysom explains the thinking further. He says it's important in any mediation to distinguish between a peace process and a constitutional reform process. 'Peace agreements are always bilateral, whereas constitutional processes are always multi-lateral. So you need to provide opportunities for other parties to be involved.' Haysom admits this has happened only to a 'limited extent' in the Sudan peace process, but the agreement does 'permit the involvement of other parties when it comes to designing the new constitution'.

The workshop in Karen, aimed at establishing workable mechanisms for the wealth-sharing protocol signed in the Naivasha agreement six months earlier, was rather like attending classes for a Masters degree in the subject. It started with a plenary session in the large assembly hall of the Karen Management Centre. The IGAD Secretariat team outlined the broad issues that the forty or so negotiators had to address, before breaking down into smaller seminar-like groups to examine specific issues in detail.

Sumbeiywo's role in this part of the process was almost cere-monial. He had simply opened the proceedings with a few words before disappearing to the side of the room to let the 'professional' mediators take over.

Sumbeiywo was no such shrinking wallflower when it came to another aspect of the mediation over which most mediators trip: the handling of the press. At the start of the process he made each party sign an agreement which allowed only Sumbeiywo to officially talk to the press about progress in the talks. Not feeling he needed a press officer himself, he ended up as the mediation's only spokesman. A spokesman who rarely spoke. 'I do not believe in mediating through the media at all. I do not have a public relations officer because that encourages the media,' Sumbeiywo explains bluntly. Did the media ever badly misreport what was going on in the process? 'Oh yes, severely. But I never corrected them.' Never? 'Never, because that would give them a story. And what people read today they have forgotten tomorrow.'

Keeping it regional

Sumbeiywo, despite the military click of his heels, has a certain earthiness when set against the remote international diplomatic interests which infused the process. It's the combination of the importance of his family, his farm and his Church. And the way he talks with paternalistic attachment about the parties. 'You have to understand that these people have been fighting for 21 years and the reason they are before you is because they trust that you will be able to help them and ease their pain. They couldn't agree anywhere, they wouldn't talk to each other, unless they were with you.' Many, particularly those from the army of diplomats which worked to push this process though, would see Sumbeiywo's belief that he was so central to this mediation as naïve.

The signing of the comprehensive peace agreement on South Sudan took place in Nairobi on 9 January 2005. Amid much diplomatic fanfare, senior politicians and dignitaries, including the US Secretary of State Colin Powell, as well as ten African heads of state and government, looked on as Sudanese Vice-President Ali Osman Taha and the SPLM/A leader John Garang grinningly waved their copies of the signed peace agreements in the air.

At this final event, the practitioners of the process had stepped aside to make way for the politicians. Many press reports of the event did not mention the organization which had run the process, IGAD. Almost none contained Lazaro Sumbeiywo's name. John Ryle is typical of many commentators on Sudan when he summed-up the process as a 'sedulous carrot-and-stick mediation by the United States'. Even the senior leadership of the parties saw it that way. John Garang, after signing the Naivasha Agreement in May 2004, told the Voice of America in a radio interview: 'This peace agreement was reached not necessarily because the parties wanted to but because both parties were forced to.'

'Forcing' parties to sign agreements has been the downfall of many a peace deal when it comes to their actual implementation. Agreements signed under pressure need constant nurturing by those who did the 'forcing'. This essential intensive care, is expensive and probably unsustainable in terms of the years of diplomatic energy and will required.

Sumbeiywo believed, however, that he kept this a regional process which would produce a workable deal. His right-hand 'men', were not the American, the British or Norwegian diplomats, but the IGAD ambassadors. Even if it did involve chucking an array of Western ambassadors out of his office in fits of rage, the international community may end up hoping that his repeated efforts to re-root the process back into the political fabric of the Horn of Africa had some effect, if only because regional mediations have a better chance of working than ones imposed from outside.

Whether or not Sumbeiywo, as he himself believed, actually ran the process, his personal style certainly affected the outcome. His defiance of the international community at times preserved the process, protected the parties, and held, however fleetingly, the mighty United States with its tendency for 'un-Sudanese' solutions to the conflict, at bay.

'You do this', he says of the international actors involved, 'by building a spider's web, to keep them in but also out'. Not an easy task. But one he accomplished with finesse even though he himself has no real taste for the political nature of such ploys. Sumbeiywo may have spent a career skimming alongside high-level politics but it was a world in which he never really belonged.

The thought of her father as a politician makes Flora laugh. 'He could never have hacked it as a politician. Politicians promise things and then don't deliver. He could never do that. And apart from anything else, he doesn't know how to lie.' She reflects for a moment. And then comes closer than anyone to explaining how a man with little time for the highly political and fickle games of international mediation, could survive them so successfully. 'Dad is such a simple man. It's hard to get the interest of a simple man. You know, fancy restaurants and gifts mean nothing to him. But his family and his cows do.'

Selected sources

Reports

International Crisis Group (ICG) 'Sudan's Dual Crisis: Refocusing on IGAD', 5 October 2004.

International Crisis Group (ICG) 'Sudan: Towards an Incomplete Peace', 11 December 2003.

International Crisis Group (ICG) 'Sudan's Best Chance for Peace, How Not to Lose It', 17 September 2002.

International Crisis Group (ICG) 'Dialogue or Destruction? Organizing for Peace as the War in Sudan Escalates', 27 June 2002.

International Crisis Group (ICG) 'God, Oil and Country: Changing the Logic of War in Sudan', January 2002.

The Danforth Report, www.state.gov/p/af/rls/rpt/10150.htm.

Jim Lobe, *Self-Determination Conflict Profile, Foreign Policy in Focus*, October 2001.

News sources

BBC News Online: Reports and analysis.

Persecution Project Foundation, 'President Bush receives Burnt Bible press release', 22 October 2002, posted on www.prayeralert.org/altertarchives/alert-02-10-02.html

John Ryle, 'Disaster in Darfur', *New York Review of Books*, 12 August 2004.

Samantha Power, 'Dying in Darfur', *New Yorker*, 30 August 2004.

www.iAbolish.org – 'President Bush Condemns Sudan for current use of Slavery in Africa', press release posted on www.warriorsfortruth.com/slavery-in-africa.html.

6 In Search of the Textbook Mediator

Antonia Potter

The art (or is it science?) of mediation in armed conflict has grown in stature to become the subject of university courses, weighty academic tomes and serious-minded 'how to' books. Former diplomats, politicians, generals, psychologists, political and social scientists, and more have downloaded the impressive sum of their combined experience and research into analysis, discourse and theory. While it must be good news that an activity the world sorely needs is getting more serious professional attention, it tends to remain obscure to the general public. Images of violent conflict continue to bombard us from news outlets, yet the conclusion is not always naturally drawn multiple from these images that where mediation is possible, and has been dared, war can be stopped – as in Bosnia or Sudan. Conversely, where the possibility of dialogue has not been allowed to gain a foothold, conflicts like Chechnya's wear bloodily on.

The new profession of mediation
In the last 15 years in particular, there has been a mediation explosion. Professionals now mediate an array of conflicts, from commercial disputes to family wrangles. With domestic law as the perennial fallback and situations most commonly involving two opposed parties whose differences are worked out privately behind a veil of confidentiality, most of these mediators operate within a tidily defined space, and are developing strong professional networks.

As the preceding chapters make all too apparent, however, the conflict mediator does not enjoy the luxury of such clarity. International law does not offer the fixed enforceability which makes national law a practical problem solver; and in armed conflict there are frequently more than two parties whose grievances need to be addressed, and who may have divergent views on how public or not they wish the process to be. Conflict mediation also operates on different levels, and with a much more self-conscious approach to power than civil mediation. The level this book has dealt with calls itself, not without a certain arrogance, 'Track One'. This track entails activity at the highest levels of rank and power, such as states or official international and regional bodies, or, less commonly, independent or private organizations with specific links to power and influence. In this track, the status of the mediator is a crucial part of the leverage brought to bear on parties who may be uninterested in reaching a negotiated settlement. Its counterpart, the more humble 'Track Two', is the activity more commonly undertaken by non-governmental organizations and community groups of building supportive constituencies for peace and initiatives for reconciliation among ordinary people. At its crudest, the distinction can be described as being between a top-down approach to making peace, and a bottom-up one.

The contributions of conflict resolution theory
The conflict resolution theory which has been developed recognizes that the context of armed conflict has a complexity all its own which makes high demands on those who confront it. As Adam Curle, the noted British mediator and grandfather of current peace studies, points out, 'There are no set answers to the problems that beset us. The historical setting, the culture, the character of the people involved, the nature of the issues concerned, demand wise and experienced, rather than textbook, treatment.'[1] He characterizes in unflattering terms the parties to what he called today's 'mini wars', describing them as 'a tangle of

phobias, cavorting egos, crazed convictions, vanity and greed'.[2] As such a description would suggest, Curle blazed the trail for a psychological approach to peace mediation theory, which has been developed by such well-known names as John Paul Lederach, Jeffery Rubin and John Burton. The approach favours analysing and deploying personality, psychology and emotion as tools, while strongly emphasizing reconciliation. For example, Rubin has provided distinctions between the types of power[3] a mediator may wield which may assist in working out how best to match mediators to the mediated. Roger MacGinty has discussed how an analysis of symbols and ritual gives unique insights into the causes and persistence of violent conflict.

In contrast to this, a rationalist school has grown up, which has directed its efforts towards analysing structural and process aspects of negotiation contexts. Proponents such as IW Zartman, Chester Crocker and William Ury have given us descriptive concepts such as ripeness and the mutually hurting stalemate as tipping points into negotiation; or appreciating different types of negotiation process as sequential, simultaneous or composite. They have provided tactical concepts such as the use of confidence-building measures to build trust between parties; helping parties to define the best alternative to a negotiated agreement or the importance of understanding how to maximize leverage within a given context. Thus both schools have gone to great lengths to describe what goes on during peace negotiations in a way which makes situations amenable to comparative analysis.

Illustrations of these concepts and many more which will be familiar to the students of this discipline emerge time and time again in the chapters of this book. The fascinating human variable of *character* is an element which theory will always find hard to capture, yet it is vital to what goes on around the negotiating table. A rationalist analysis of such negotiations is likely to describe institutions and positions pitted against each other; the more psychologically minded approach will depict a group of characters and relationships. Neither description, of course, has a monopoly on the truth. Yet character and relationships certainly have a way of reinterpreting institutions, and reconfiguring rules and lessons. They can act as the alchemist element in a situation which might otherwise remain untransformed.

The confluence of theory and practice

By telling the story of six mediators, this book has illustrated how mediation theory and practice combine and sometimes collide with character in the real-life drama – although often of a desperately slow and frustrating kind – of conflict resolution. It has revealed the unpredictable and sometimes counter-intuitive combinations of skills, experience and personal attributes that have brought each of these individuals to the pinnacle of a mysterious and unorthodox career path. And it has confronted us with the fact that none of these mediators, perhaps some of the best known names in the field today, have studied or purport to refer to the body of theory which exists.

Fellow practitioners, teachers, students and followers of politics and international relations, even the subjects of mediation themselves, will have found much that they recognize in the practice of these six mediators. They will have seen the full arsenal of recognized techniques in mediation on display, and perhaps even have recognized new ones. They may have mused on whether a different mediator might have achieved other results in a given situation. They will have observed without surprise that black and white designations of success and failure prove hopelessly unsubtle judgements on the results of the mediators' work: peace agreements of a kind may be hammered out (for example Afghanistan's Bonn 2001 Agreement or the 2002 Aceh Cessation of Hostilities Agreement) but may well fall apart when put into practice. This could be the result of pressures both inherent in the agreement itself, like the failure to plan for neutralizing opponents who might bring down the process by violence, or relating to factors which play beyond its parameters, like the negative behaviour of hostile neighbours, or simply insufficient money to finance expensive ceasefire monitoring, security and confidence-building projects.

So, given the diversity of issues and situations provided in this snapshot of selected mediations, has the book offered a template for what might make the textbook conflict mediator?

The role of the mediator

We might first ask ourselves what such a third party conflict mediator actually does. Simply put, they try to establish peace out of conflict, hopefully a peace that lasts. They are not one of the protagonists, and must work with all parties to the conflict to find a workable solution to their differences, and if possible, to prepare them for putting that solution into practice. The general model is to run talks designed to culminate in an agreement that all parties are willing to sign, and for the implementation of which sufficient political will and resources have been ensured. But, of course, getting to the stage where talks are even possible is a breakthrough in itself. Talks about the main issue may be preceded by months or even years of talks about those talks. These might be formal, open talks, or secret sessions, or both in parallel. They involve wrangling over matters like who is represented and at what level, what is on and off the agenda, where and when the meeting will be and how participation will be funded, any and all of which can stop a fledgling process dead in its tracks if it goes the wrong way. There are a range of challenges the mediator needs to handle: a key one is how you include *personae non gratae* in any kind of official talks. Not only may the government in question regard some or all opposing elements in the conflict as outlaws – and often terrorists – but other important governments may too. On top of that, how can the mediator establish that the groups putting themselves forward do in fact represent the people that they claim to?

The mediator's boss

The mediator's own institutional home will affect how they respond to these challenges. They are responsible to someone –

perhaps to the UN like de Soto and Brahimi; to a regional organization like Sumbeiywo; to the board of a private foundation like Griffiths; or to a government like Helgesen and Solheim. Their formal accountability to the parties and the people they claim to represent is by honour only, dictated by the diplomatic requirements of their institutional home and their personal interpretation of those. This is the nature of being the third party; as Griffiths says with unblinking honesty, 'it's not my people who are suffering' – although in the case of the regional mediator, those people might well be their neighbours. The mediator may have been appointed, but in some cases, it may seem as though he made the appointment himself; after all, they are no mediator worth their salt if they do not know about making and taking advantage of being in the right place at the right time.

Their institutional home is significant: the smaller and less formal the institution which backs them, the more room they have for manoeuvre especially at the early stages of a process, but the less effective the carrots and sticks they have to apply at critical junctures. Where it is impossible for the UN, or a major government like the US to speak to declared or suspected terrorists like Aceh's GAM, or Sri Lanka's Tamil Tigers, Griffiths' Centre for Humanitarian Dialogue, or the non-EU government of the Norwegian duo are able to be in contact with groups who do not have the status of governments, and who may be moral and legal outcasts from some national or international regimes. The mediators' response to the charge that one should not talk to suspected international criminals such as these groups tends to be that it is not for the mediator to pass judgement, but to create a situation where issues like accountability for crimes committed might properly be handled at some future point.

It seems our textbook conflict mediator – and this applies even to UN mediators – must be willing to live with what might kindly be described as moral ambiguity. They must be prepared to talk to and even befriend those whose hands may be stained with blood. There is not a mediator in this book who has not had a moment where they have asked themselves whether they are complicit in a fraudulent process. It is their lonely judgement, in the end, which will answer the question for them.

The omnipresent United States of America

Their institutional home will also define the resources they can bring to bear on the situation. The relative force of the moral and financial pressure they can apply will vary from situation to situation. Brahimi, in Iraq, had the authority of his experience, stature and UN backing undercut by American manoeuvring. Sumbeiywo's IGAD process in Sudan was at a standstill until the US intervened. As the latter examples demonstrate, the most powerful institution in play may well not be the mediator's own, and they may find themselves spending more time managing a relationship with that institution than servicing their own. Almost always, the most significant such actor will be the US: its priorities, its approaches, its obsessions and its neglects continue to provide the great rock in the ocean around which the waters of international relations flow. In all the mediations described here, bar Cyprus, US interests, in particular with regard to the war on terror, have loomed large. Our mediator will always need to keep an eye on the American interest if they want their ball to remain in play.

A member of the international elite

As with many jobs at the top of the tree, being able to demonstrate a specialism in each country in question is never essential, even if desirable for the textbook mediator. Their familiarity with the situation of conflict may be deep and personal, acquired through experience or interest or their impressive, carefully cultivated network of contacts; or it may develop opportunistically with their appointment to the position. For them, absorbing the complexities of history and politics that lead countries and territories to the brink of the abyss is a natural consequence of their privileged education, their time as a leader or in high office, their keen interest in politics, their life on the international scene, the research and analysis skills of their staff. Although not each mediator in this book can lay claim to all these happy attributes, even the humblest of them has been privileged to some extent in terms of the opportunities life has provided them, and what they have been able to do with them. Those that consider themselves the least privileged tend to present themselves as the least sophisticated. For the Norwegians, Helgesen and Solheim, simplicity is an integral part of their self-image and self-justification for involving themselves in other people's business. Sumbeiywo, perhaps the mediator with the least international profile in this book, is often described as having a naïve approach (though many would argue his straightforwardness masks a keen grasp of the power plays). He is the only one of the six to have led an army, an experience that infuses his brooks-no-insubordination style. By contrast, Brahimi, who is as patrician as his UN colleague de Soto is cosmopolitan, is the only one to be able to boast hard political experience as a revolutionary in his native Algeria. The one with the most informal style – Griffiths – has had correspondingly the most experience of working outside the world of government and the UN. Most of them have diplomatic credentials. All of them are networkers *extraordinaire*.

The lack of women mediators

The mediator seems likely, then, to be a member of an elite, the kind of person whose good offices as an eminent person might be requested in a number of ways by leaders with problems to solve, either at home, next door or far away. But does that require the mediator to be a 'he'? It cannot go without remark that this book profiles six men, nor that, to date, almost none of the most noteworthy senior mediators have been women. The continuing exclusion from and under-representation of women in public life in the large majority of nations is reflected in the UN's system, and must in large part be responsible for this glaring deficit. To bring the point home in the context of the world body for peace-making: in 2005, of the United Nations Secretary General's 61 special and personal representatives and envoys and their deputies engaged on specifically peace-related work, there are four women.[4] Yet women such as Margaret Anstee (Secretary General's Special Representative to Angola in 1992–93, as part of a distinguished UN career), or Betty Bigombe (a former Ugandan Minister who became a mediator between Uganda's government and the Lord's Resistance Army in the north of the country) have managed to break through and work in mediating roles, proving that it is not impossible. The comparative roles that men and women have played and could play in brokering peace is a significant research area which merits more attention. Research and anecdote suggest that women have been considerably and powerfully more active at the grassroots in community-based peace-building and reconciliation activities, the so-called 'Track Two' stream of peace-making work. This activity is indispensable and awe-inspiring. But it is also patronizing to assume that its nature and extent is enough to explain women's absence from senior positions in official peace-related functions. The explanation of this absence remains reprehensibly unexplored and any possible response to it correspondingly lacking – in this book as elsewhere.

The drive to mediate

While this can only remain speculation, it is still important – and irresistible – to ask what motivates the mediator. Mediation is disruptive to a settled life, as unpredictable, demanding and unreasonable as a spoiled child. Griffiths' 13 trips to Jakarta and Stockholm in 2002, de Soto's marathon attendance of almost 50 meetings before making his first move, Brahimi's through-the-night meetings, are part of the mediators' deeply unglamorous stock in trade, and hardly, in themselves, pastimes to aspire to. Undoubtedly, all six mediators are true believers in peace, but this simple, unarguable belief hardly puts them in exclusive company. They may profess that talking is always better than the recourse to force, but none of them would rule out the need for force in ensuring international security under certain circumstances. Undoubtedly, they are people of a certain ego – an attribute often unfairly maligned, without which most significant acts on the world stage would be hard to achieve. Without exception, they all claim humility. But it is hard to imagine that none of them has ever been visited in the night by fleeting dreams of a Nobel Peace Prize. Mediation is an odd sop to the ego: it is to have great power, potentially, and yet no power at all. For Helgesen and Solheim, they simply look to 'be of use'. Griffiths suggests dryly that it all comes down to giving mother something to be proud of. They are all to some extent spellbound by politics and the potential power of mediation. Sumbeiywo is alone in his twin assertions that he finds no enjoyment in conflict mediation, and that the only thing he fears is God.

A smorgasbord of tactics

What skills do mediators need to pursue this tricky task? They may not care to use the terminology of theory, but they will have an impressive array of tactics on hand. They know how to exploit timing, stalemates and windows of opportunity to their advantage. They can keep things on track by excluding explosive topics from certain stages of the talks, and thereby slowly building trust. They can keep new or important ideas in play without stalling the progress of the main talks by setting up proximity talks which run in parallel. They might refuse to let a meeting end on a bad note, or without a plan for the next meeting. They can keep their delegates up all night, refusing even to go to the bathroom so that the pressure is literally kept on to reach conclusions. They may put their arm around one leader while strolling in the garden, or talk family matters with another in the sauna or the jacuzzi. They can confine the lead negotiators in a room with a deadline to emerge with an agreement. They might relentlessly invite the teams out for dinner after dinner, or despatch them off for supervised woodland walks like an earnest parent. They can encourage them to ventilate their feelings and frustrations like a therapist. They may lose their temper, deliberately or without guile; or refuse ever to be ruffled. They might have the parties submit position papers and then supervise as they hammer them into a single unified document, or they may present them with their own comprehensive document and require them to work through it clause by clause. Cunning as a fox, they will have thought through the angles of how to keep the process secret and deniable where necessary. They might use the trappings and resources of their position as bribery: my government will only fund the process if this condition is met, the international community will only give its blessing to the agreement if that criterion is satisfied. They perform a dual function, both conduit and shield, ensuring that interested observers have appropriate access, either overtly or otherwise, to influence the protagonists, or are prevented from doing so; sometimes, it may seem, they are barely involved in the mediation at all, but presiding over it like a godfather while a contracted-in team of negotiation specialists does the actual business of running the talking shop.

Communication is everything

Language skills matter. They are likely to need fluent English alongside their other tongues. But if they can boast one or more of the native tongues of the parties, so much the better. In Sri Lanka, the participation of the LTTE at meetings is often defined more by English language proficiency than by the organizational ranking or power of the participants. The bond a person feels to a stranger who can speak their native language cannot be overestimated. And the fact that discussions will frequently descend to tussles over single words, their meanings and their translation, mean that the mediator's grasp of the situation will be exponentially strengthened if they are master at this level of semantic and linguistic nuance.

Their communication skills must include an ability to handle the press. They may have to face a vigorous and partisan national press, and an international media which is either obsessively

fascinated or elaborately bored by the process they are mas-
terminding. The role of the media in peace-making, and the
capacities of mediators in strategic handling of the media are
important subjects that the mediations in this book suggest are
under-explored. Each of these mediations imply that, far from
simply reporting the process, the media often makes itself a protagonist, forcing developments through the timing and substance
of frequently leaked nuggets of information. Press speculation
over Brahimi's picks for the Iraqi Interim Governing Council
combined with US machinations derailed his carefully laid plans.
The Sri Lankan press is notoriously partisan, and the Norwegians
have learnt to accept it as an obstacle on the peace process's
torturous path. Perhaps it is not surprising, then, that mediators
are likely to be very suspicious of the media: Sumbeiywo refuses
all media contact, even to correct them when they publish factual
errors; Griffiths, like Brahimi, claims discomfort, even disdain, in
the face of the press, but knows that the information he controls
and imparts is another weapon in his often lightweight armoury.

Management: boon or burden?
The higher up any hierarchy one climbs, the harder it is to avoid
the burden of management responsibility. The mediator is no
different, though none of the six evince a great love of the task.
They have a team to support them, to whom as likely as not they
become very close. But they frustrate them, often preferring to
work alone; or confuse them, alternating apparent neglect of their
reasonable needs and claims as employees and colleagues with
tender consideration for their health and welfare and that of their
family. They may have an inner circle to whom all trust and
solicitude is extended, but beyond whose cosy confines staff
languish resentful or bewildered in the cold. They may find
themselves running a political mission, a whole multi-faceted
operation of which the mediation effort forms only one, if vital,
part, but the part that receives the lion's share of their attention.
They may have another job entirely – running a foundation, a

government department, an army – which will make its demands on them from time to time, with a certain plaintive futility. As far as support for themselves, they may seek it – both practically and morally – from the boss, their partners, or even God. Or from no one at all.

Building popular support for the peace process

A final skill they would do well to command is the capacity to identify ways of building the popular support of ordinary people for the peace process. This is clearly linked to the challenge of establishing whether the conflict parties are sufficiently representative of the communities in question, and it is perhaps one of the most labour-intensive and tough areas in which to achieve success, as well as the one least suited to the elite mediator. Peace agreements carve up power and wealth and work out arrangements for issues with enormous impact on people's daily lives, like security and justice. If they cannot capture an element of what the average citizen aspires to, their chances of failure are that much greater. But it is not impossible to ignore the time-consuming business of finding out what the average citizen thinks, when you are already faced with the exhausting prospect of a bringing a roomful of angry leaders to some kind of lasting consensus. Thus, while each of the six mediators would undoubtedly, if to varying degrees, recognize the importance of this civil society buy-in, they have tended not to prioritize it.

The private mediator

As to the personal attributes of conflict mediators, this sample, slender though it is, suggests there is no mediation personality type. They may, however, share some motifs. For example, a thick skin is useful. If things even reach that stage, no sooner than a deal is signed, all manner of people will start picking holes in it: they will complain it ignores the interests of a critically important group, or it shies away from a vital issue like how the crimes of the conflict will be dealt with, or it merely postpones dealing with the real problems; insufficient resources and other political obstacles may mean it is not implemented fully, or in the way that was intended. Beneath this thick skin, the mediator is likely to embody a curious cocktail of patience, determination, humility and self-belief. Whether they make that cocktail their own with the addition of further ingredients like charm, temper, guile, imagination, humour, directness, rudeness or *politesse* rests between them and their maker.

Tomorrow's mediator

As Curle reminded us, a textbook is no use without judgement as to its application. And no training course, even at the most high-end institution, will provide the indefinable impetus to the development of judgement that the blend of character – intelligence and experience does. While theory is undoubtedly valuable in tracking and describing how the conflict mediator gets the job done, and what obstacles they face in doing so, it inevitably lacks the predictive power to tell us how to pick the right man – or woman – for the next job that comes up. So, despite the fact that they themselves are not steeped in mediation theory, there is much to learn from the practice of these six conflict mediators. And given that they remain too preoccupied fighting today's fires to worry about tomorrow's, it is perhaps through vivid accounts like these that the practitioners, analysts and theorists who will face tomorrow's crop of armed conflicts will have their best chance of reaping the lessons of their combined experience.

Notes

1   Dylan Mathews (ed), forewords, Elise Boulding and Adam Curle; Introduction, Scilla Elworthy. *War Prevention Works: 50 Stories of People Resolving Conflict*, Oxford: Oxford Research Group, 2001. Available from www.oxfordresearch group.org.uk.
2   Adam Curle, *Another Way: Positive response to contemporary violence*, Oxford: Jon Carpenter Publishing, 1995, p. 64.

3   For example, he identifies coercive, reward, expert, legitimate, referent and informational power.
4   Their various titles and current list can be found at www.un.org/News/ossg/srsg/table.htm. The women currently holding the four offices referred to are: Swiss Heidi Tagliavini (SRSG Georgia since July 2002); Canadian Carolyn McAskie (SRSG Burundi since June 2004); Bangladeshi Ameeerah Haq (DSRSG Afghanistan since June 2004); and Patricia Waring-Ripley (DSRSG Kosovo since August 2005).

This chapter drew on the following sources

Barnes, Catherine, 'Owning the process: public participation in peacemaking', *Accord*, Issue 13, Conciliation Resources, 2002.

Cahill, Kevin M (ed), *Preventive Diplomacy: stopping wars before they start*, Routledge, 2000.

Cohen, Raymond, *Negotiating Across Cultures: International communication in an interdependent world*, USIP, 2004 (revised edition).

Crocker, Chester A, Hampton, Fen Osler and Aall, Pamela (eds), *Turbulent Peace: The challenges of managing international conflict*, USIP, 2001.

Crocker, Chester A, Hampton, Fen Osler and Aall, Pamela (eds), *Herding Cats: Multiparty mediation in a complex world*, USIP 1999.

Darby, John and MacGinty, Roger (eds), *Contemporary Peacemaking: Conflict, violence and peace processes*, Palgrave Macmillan, 1993.

El Buhra, Judy, *Women Building Peace, Sharing Know How*, International Alert, 2003.

Hall, Lavinia (ed), *Negotiation: Strategies for mutual gain*, Sage Publications, 1993.

Harris, Peter and Riley, Ben (eds), *Democracy and Deep-Rooted Conflict: Options for negotiatiors*, International IDEA Handbook Series 3, International IDEA, 1998.

Rehn, Elisabeth and Sirleaf Ellen Johnson, *Women, War and Peace: The independent expert's assessment on the impact of armed conflict on women and women's role in peace-building*, UNIFEM, 2002.

Stedman, Stephen John; Rothchild, Donald and Cousens, Elizabeth M (eds), *Ending Civil Wars: The implementation of peace agreements*, Lynne Rienner, 2002.

War-torn Societies Project, *Rebuilding after War: Lessons from the War-torn Societies Project*, 1999.

Zartman, I. William and Rasmussen, J. Lewis (eds), *Peacemaking in International Conflicts: Methods and techniques*, USIP, 1997.

Acknowledgements

The author

The dedicated staff on whom each of these mediators depend were exceptionally helpful to me in researching this book. I am indebted to those at the Royal Norwegian Ministry of Foreign Affairs, the IGAD secretariat and the United Nations without whose help each of these chapters would have been considerably thinner. Thanks too to Elizabeth Cousens, Jilla Moazami, Maria Myles, Phillip Winter and the Center for Research on Audio-visual Sources of History, HEI, Geneva. Also to Jane Munge of the Jesuit Refugee Service in Nairobi and all the refugees from South Sudan who gave me their views on the peace process.

I would also like to thank Esra Yagiz for the her endless help in researching this book; Becky Abrams, Claudia McGoldrick and John Ryle for their suggestions; Paula Murphy Ives for her knowledge of conflict resolution; Pam Hughes for lifelong advice on writing; and editing and Ben Martin for being always there to help when things did not work. And my ever indebted thanks to my friend and au pair Lenka Kurucova without whom this book would have not have got written and/or my children would not have been fed. And, finally, my love and thanks always to my husband Mark, for his support, his patience and for always giving the best advice.

Working with the Centre of Humanitarian Dialogue was tremendous fun and I have to thank for that Andy Andrea, David Petrasek, Hugo Slim and especially Antonia Potter who nurtured this book with the patience and love of a first-class midwife.

Acknowledgements

The Centre for Humanitarian Dialogue
The Centre for Humanitarian Dialogue would like to thank all those who helped in the preparation of this book, not least the six mediators who are profiled for giving so generously of their time, and for their willingness to share their thoughts and feelings. In addition, we are particularly grateful to our funders, and the Royal Norwegian Ministry of Foreign Affairs deserves special thanks in this regard.

Finally we are very grateful to the author, Harriet Martin, whose fresh and independent voice and insight have turned a dry project idea for understanding the experiences of senior conflict mediators into an engaging and vivid book, of interest and relevance to the wider audience of those who are interested in the causes of war and the makings of peace.

Geneva
October 2005

Index

military level
  Aceh, Indonesia 66, 77, 78, 79, 86–7, 95, 98
  Afghanistan 16, 21
  Cyprus 31, 62
  Lazaro Sumbeiywo 138, 145–6, 166
  Southern Sudan 144
Millington, Jeff 148
Moi, Daniel arap 145
monitoring roles 90–91
Moragoda, Milinda 112, 114, 120, 121
moral ambiguity 164–5
motivations to mediate 167–8

NAD *see* Nanggroe Aceh Darussalem law
Naivasha talks 150–53
Nakuru document 146–9
Nanggroe Aceh Darussalem (NAD) law 77, 81
nationalism 54
navigation by sight 4
neutrality 75, 84, 107
New Prevention thesis 75
New York meeting 44–8, 60
Nicosia 48–50
No campaign 55–6, 61–2, 62–3
Norway
  criticism 115–16, 117–18, 129
  exclusion 125
  roles 101–2, 103–5, 112–13
  straight-talking approaches 121–2, 166
  terrorism 164
  withdrawal 119–20

observers 16–137, 140–46, 148
oil industry 69–70, 78–80, 81–2, 137

Omar, Mullah 15
opening ceremony protocol 110–111
Oxi *see* No campaign

Pachachi, Adnan 9–10
Page, Susan 142, 143, 144
Pakistan 17
Papadopoulos, Tassos 33, 42–3, 46–7, 51–4, 55, 59
Papapetrou, Michaelis 34–5, 36
parliamentary elections 24
Patten, Chris 116
perceptions 58, 62–3, 74, 77, 123, 171
Perdikis, George 51
personae non gratae 163
Pfirter, Didier 41
political level 14–15, 104–5, 110, 117–20, 123, 157
Powell, Colin 153, 156
power 73–4, 161
power-sharing protocols 1, 20, 39, 150
Prabhakaran, Velupillai 109–10, 116
practical level 162–3, 172
preparatory meetings 139–40, 163
presidential level
  Afghanistan 24
  Iraq interim governments 9–10
  Sri Lanka 108, 110, 117, 118–19
prime ministerial level 8–9, 108, 118–19, 120
private mediators 67–9
professional level 159–60
property rights 36, 62
psychological approaches 161
Puleedevan, Seevarathnam 113, 124

Printed in the United Kingdom
by Lightning Source UK Ltd.
124048UK00001B/31/A

9 780826 490575